I0069795

The Chief Executive's
Survival Kit

BY DR. DAVID J. GOODWILL

The Chief Executive's
Survival Kit

BY DR. DAVID J. GOODWILL

Published By Dr. D. J. Goodwill

Photographs by Dr. Sharon D. Goodwill

**Printed in the United States of America
Second Edition, 2014
ISBN: 978-0692-01342-7**

The Chief Executive's Survival Kit

About the Author

Dr. David J. Goodwill has over 25 years of leadership experience as President and CEO of multi-company divisions of four different international corporations throughout the USA and Europe. He has a track record of results enhancement and restoring ventures to growth and profitability in a wide range of different industries in both manufacturing and service environments. He has supervised a large number of acquisitions and disposals, has restructured operations involving strategic rationalization and plant closures, has been involved in several successful start-ups, and has overseen many major capital projects through to fruition.

Dr. Goodwill is an experienced practitioner of Total Quality Management and a keen advocate of lean manufacturing. Throughout his distinguished career, he recognized that the challenge of developing an appropriate and recognizable culture within the organization was one of his prime tasks as the CEO.

His education includes a Bachelor degree with honors in Natural Sciences and a Ph.D. achieved at age 26 both from the University of Cambridge in England. He gained a Diploma in Management Studies from Sheffield Polytechnic, where he graduated as the top student in his year. He was an external examiner and adviser to three British business schools. Until retirement, he was a fellow of the British Institute of Management and served on their National Education Committee.

INTRODUCTION

Being a CEO is a bit like being a plumber. A plumber fixes leaks, installs new equipment, and makes complex systems work effectively. If a plumber has served an effective apprenticeship, knows what he is doing, and cares a lot about the quality of his work, he will do a good job. He will please his customers and feel good at the end of the day when he goes home. If he is short on skills, sooner or later there will be a problem. No one is going to benefit from his labors in the long run. If he is incompetent, watch out because disaster is just around the corner.

Just as with plumbers, CEOs fix leaks in company earning potential, invest in new equipment, and manage complex systems. Untrained and incompetent plumbers are out there. Untrained and incompetent CEOs are even more abundant. Are you about to become one? If you have any doubt about this, you should read and study this book.

Just as the plumber carries with him a bag of essential tools of his trade, so, too, should the CEO. Many of the most useful are included here.

Brief Description of the book

This book is about how to be a Chief Executive Officer. It contains a great deal of original material that the author has developed himself as a practicing CEO with 25 years experience and as a keen student of the science of management. It contains checklists that you will not find anywhere else. It also describes a lot of well-tried tools and techniques and management practices on which the author has put his own slant based on many years of experience using them. This makes them more practical and much easier to use. The book is unique in that it covers the majority of the important things that a CEO will need in a very readable and workable format. Taken as a whole it represents a career's worth of learning how to be a successful CEO and how to master all of the many facets that this special job entails.

When a CEO takes on a new assignment, what should they do and in what order? What do they need to know? These questions are answered in a logical series of sections. Diagrams and charts are used where this assists understanding. As the

title suggests, it is intended as a comprehensive "Chief Executive's Survival Kit" presented in places as checklists.

Most managers know how to get to the point where they have a plan. That's the easy bit. The thing that differentiates the world class manager from others is that they know how to make that plan happen. The best way is to use a systematic process of deploying the company's goals throughout the whole organization. In this way, every employee appreciates how what they do fits into the overall scheme of things. This is empowering and motivating to employees so that they will want to achieve their part. When everyone is facing in the same direction and each knows what they have to do and has the power to do it, no challenge is too great for the organization!

Who is the book intended for?

This book is intended for all CEOs as they move through their careers into new and bigger positions. It will be especially useful and is a "must read" for business school graduates and CEOs who have just landed their first general management position, since it provides a comprehensive approach to the CEO function. When you become a CEO, you are only given a limited amount of time to decide what you must do to improve the enterprise that you have joined and to begin to add significant value in your new role. If you miss something important early on, it will return to haunt you. You therefore need to be very organized. The approach presented here has been tried and tested many times over. The tools and checklists are invaluable and they all work if applied properly.

ACKNOWLEDGEMENTS

I should like to thank my lovely wife, Sharon, for editing this book and providing the photographs, and for giving me her patience and the love and inspiration to finish the book.

I should also like to thank Judy Suiter for providing the necessary guidance and information on self-publishing.

TABLE OF CONTENTS

Chapter   **Page**

| **Chapter 1** | **Getting Started** |

Getting People's Attention

In any organization that receives a new leader, there will be those who welcome the change and those who are more cynical. If you come with a good track record, show early on that you are dynamic and committed you will get your people's attention. In many cases, especially where you are replacing someone who was relieved of their position (as opposed to being promoted, for example), there will be a palpable sigh of relief as you fill the leadership vacuum. This is the best of situations because it gives you the whole stage on which to perform. Contrariwise, you may be following the rising star who had transformed the business, grown it almost beyond measure, and has now just been promoted. This can be more challenging and requires a little more nerve and self-assurance to create a new leadership platform, especially where the previous incumbent becomes your new boss. It can be very challenging to be in a job where your boss knows significantly more about your job initially than you do.

Make a Personal Statement

From the moment that you arrive, people will be watching your every move for signs and signals as to how to behave. They want to please you and to know how to please and impress you. Show them. Give them the signs and signals. Do it consciously, not unconsciously. Think about it. Plan it. Only then will you do it well and consistently.

Look good, feel good, and sound good!

Dress in the manner that you want your senior managers to dress, but always look well turned out. It is my experience that your people expect you to look like their leader. Carry yourself with a demeanor that you would wish your colleagues to mimic. Feel good about yourself. Being the leader is fun. Along with the responsibility and accountability, the job gives you great privileges so enjoy them. This is the profession that you have chosen for yourself, so become good at it. When you talk in

6

public, prepare well and always sound good. People will expect you to be good at public speaking so practice it and learn to enjoy doing it. If you find it difficult and a chore you may be in the wrong profession since the ability to communicate well to all and sundry is the most important requirement of your job.

Modus Operandi

Make it clear from the start how you want to operate, what are the rules, what is acceptable and what is unacceptable. Do it with aplomb. Appear to be casual (but plan every move carefully). Use a little humor to put in place the toughest changes.

Setting the Pace

You need to demonstrate great energy and exude confidence. Both are very contagious. You will find that your team will readily adapt its pace of doing things to match that set by you. If you are slow and pedantic, so will they be. If you set a cracking pace from the moment you arrive, everyone will feel and respond to your sense of urgency. Your team will look to you to take on the mantle of leadership and to have confidence in your own ability. If you haven't, you're in the wrong job.

Give your Troops an Early Victory

If you can, find an area that affects a large proportion of the workforce, management and employees, in terms of their working environment and conditions. Ideally it will be one that the previous administration has clearly and to everyone's knowledge failed to address satisfactorily. **Then nail it**!

Do check with your leadership team carefully that this will not have serious repercussions that you have not thought of and get their buy-in. This will send the strongest possible message that here is a new leader who is decisive and clearly more effective than what went before, and has the employee's best interests at heart. Ideally it will be something that doesn't cost too much and has a psychological impact much greater than the cost.

One example that I inherited was where for years there was inadequate space to park and people never knew when they came to work whether they would find a space. Worse still, because of the cramped conditions, people were also continually

getting dents and dings in their doors from careless parkers. Creating more space by repaving and relaying out of the car park was a very visible action that affected everyone beneficially and significantly reduced two major areas of daily annoyance.

Contrariwise, the worst thing that you can do early on in your administration is to remove a significant amenity under the guise of cost cutting. This will do much more damage to morale and your company's results than the cost saving. It will also not endear you to your workforce, and everything from then on will be uphill. An example that I came across involving a former colleague was to close the company restaurant. Not a good first move on his part!

I am not recommending here that you go out of your way to seek popularity as a leader, but simply that you recognize that as the new CEO, all eyes are on you and you need to retain their attention in the most positive way from the outset. You will, for sure, need to make decisions that people will not like but they will understand and go along with you if they see that you demonstrate a balanced approach and are on their side and have their best interests in mind.

A Note on Company Restaurants

If you are lucky enough to have one in your factory or office these days, don't close it if you can possibly avoid it. It seems such an easy cost cutting initiative. But the value that your organization gets by people being able to come together during the day to chat and get to know one another cannot be over stated. Make sure that management mixes with staff and employees at lunchtime. This is a unique opportunity for the organization to get together as one body in one place.

Breakfasts and "brown bag" lunches

If you have a company restaurant, use it to hold breakfasts and lunches with your employees at least once per week in groups of about ten or twelve...no managers present except you. If you do not have a canteen, you can order in sandwiches from a local supplier for what we call the "brown bag" lunch. If you have more than 500 employees, help them do the math and explain to them that they may expect to dine with you only about once per year. I usually start by telling them that anything they tell me will not be

attributable and that they can speak feely. Then I usually ask them "What's wrong with this organization?". People just love to tell the Chief Executive! So listen.

Be a Good Listener

It is essential that you be a good listener. It is also very important that you cultivate the reputation of being a good listener. Ask people what they think. Talk to everyone in the organization. Then people will share with you their innermost thoughts and you will benefit from experience from a wide cross section of the organization. You will begin to acquire people's trust when you are seen to act on something that people have told you, and you make it clear to everyone that you are taking this action because it was brought to your attention by an employee. If you do not intend to take action on a particular point that someone raises, explain to them why not. Don't leave the issue open in their mind. When they see that their views count, people from all over the organization will open up and confer with you about their likes and dislikes and give you their honest opinions. This is a wonderful source of ideas to be tapped by the intelligent new CEO

Be on the look out for solutions and don't be surprised where they come from. Sometimes the lowliest person in the workforce has a great solution to a challenge that the organization has been facing that lay untapped because they were never asked.

Be seen to be Democratic as well as Autocratic

The right balance between being democratic and autocratic is difficult to achieve. However, in the most general terms you should be seen to be democratic on occasions that merit debate and consensus-building and autocratic in areas where decisiveness is essential or where you wish to make a statement. Don't make the mistake of being too democratic. Meetings will go on far too long and you will be seen to be weak. People look to their leaders for decisions and action.

The Company Council

One good way to arrange to receive input from all levels of the organization on issues in the workplace that affect everyone (except those related to pay and rations, company strategy, etc.) is to form a company council with a democratically elected

representative from each department or work area. Council members are responsible for bringing issues to put before the council from employees in their work area and communicating back decisions of the council. You should chair the council personally and have your people person **Facilitate** the meetings (see later chapter on "Meetings Management"). The council should discuss the issues and make recommendations to management to implement change. In your position as CEO, you can choose to influence the outcome of these deliberations to a greater or lesser extent depending on the issue. Don't go to the council meeting without a formal agenda and knowing where you want the meeting to end up on each issue. Your people person should lobby council members in advance to influence its members if it is important to you that you get a particular result. This is exactly how government works only on a smaller scale.

It is my experience that the company council is much more aggressive about bringing about change than your management team would or could be, and you have a ready made vehicle for communicating decisions of the council back to the workforce. The best example I have was where the previous management had sweated long and hard on the issue of smoking in or near the workplace. Since many people smoked at that time, management knew that they had a real issue on their hands. The council we had established dealt with this issue on or about its second meeting, since it was high on its priority list. Because the process was seen to be democratic and coming from its own council and not from management, the edict to stop smoking in the workplace was decided and implemented without so much as a murmur from the workforce. Also, the plan to create special outside, sheltered areas for smokers to go to at break time was implemented quickly and effectively. For me it was a classic exercise in how to do things the right way within an organization.

Encourage the Team Players / Deal Swiftly with the Blockers

Within your starting lineup of managers there will be several players who really want you to succeed and want to give you all the help that they can. They will be obvious to you because their behavior will demonstrate loyalty and a consistently helpful approach. Use these people to the full. They may not be the brightest or most capable people in your leadership group, but in

the beginning, you will need all of the loyalty and help that you can get. Interestingly, at a later stage when you have decided what skills you need in your leadership group, they may be on the transfer list. That's OK, too, so long as you reward their early loyalty in some special way and get them into a position that plays to their particular strengths.

There are those who will try to resist changes that you want to implement. There are some whose attitude towards change is inappropriate. We call them "blockers". There may even be some that challenge you openly within your management group in an unconstructive way. Talk with them outside of the meeting. If they persist, fire them. If head office thinks highly of them, get them to take them off your hands and relocate them elsewhere in the organization. If your boss values them, make him accept the problem by putting them somewhere else in **his or her** organization. In any event, get them off your radar screen so that they cease to be a problem for you. You have far too much to get done to have to worry about people who will slow down the progress of change, or worse still become a destructive element that will affect the cohesiveness of your management team.

Dealing with blockers usually involves decisions that are fairly easy to make and getting rid of blockers will do wonders in focusing the rest of team. They will be as glad as you are that an unhelpful and negative element in the team has been removed and that everyone can now get on with the business. They will also be impressed by your decisiveness. And you will get their attention in a way that is really quite helpful!

Do's and Don'ts

A number of general points have been covered so far. Specific "Do's and Don'ts" are listed in Checklist Number 1.

Checklist Number 1 - Do's and Don'ts

DO:

1. Get a really good Chief Financial Officer; you're going to need this above all else.

2. Follow your instincts and your visceral ("gut") feel; if you are going to be any good as a CEO these need to be keenly developed.

3. Listen and encourage people to state their opinions; you cannot do this CEO job alone.

4. Be courageous and bold and address the tough issues first; they will fester and do damage if not addressed head on.

5. Make controlled experiments and take manageable risks; no risk no reward.

6. Build a leadership team of really strong players and delegate to the fullest; then you can focus on being a CEO.

7. Discover quickly who is with you and who is not; if they're not get rid of them.

8. Understand fully your brief; this is what you will be measured on.

9. Be pro-active in telling your boss regularly what is happening; if you don't he may assume nothing is happening (this is human nature).

10. Insure that there are no surprises; it demonstrates more control over a situation to communicate bad news in advance of an event than afterwards.

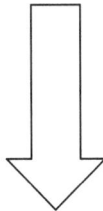

DO: (continued)

11. Pace yourself; this is a middle distance race not a sprint.

12. Keep yourself fit and get plenty of exercise whenever you can; the unfit lion loses the pride.

13. Take time out to think; being ahead in the intellectual stakes is part of what you get paid for.

14. Never lie; the truth is so much easier to handle in the long run.

15. Always be consistent; inconsistent leaders are regarded as "flakey".

16. Develop political smarts in all directions; if you're doing your job well, you **will** make detractors and even some enemies.

17. Know your industry better than anyone else; if you do this and are intelligent you will become invincible.

18. Join trade bodies and committees to find out what is going on with your competitors; this will help to keep you externally focused.

19. Visit your key accounts regularly; they are flattered to receive "royal visits" from the CEO of their supplier and you will learn a lot from spending time with your customers.

20. Communicate with employees at every opportunity what it is that you are trying to do; if they know, they can help you and they will because it's in their interest that you succeed.

21. Be punctual and demand punctuality from others; everyone perceives their time as valuable so respect this.

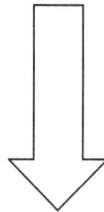

DO: (continued)

22. Don't let anything knock you off course except your boss and your own re-evaluation of the situation; everything will conspire to try to distract you, only your resolve will prevent this.

23. Use consultants only when you really need them; manage them closely and be sure to get value.

24. Have a sense of humor especially when it comes to the really tough decisions; attaining a true balance of gravity and levity will gain respect.

25. Celebrate successes though they be small; this will do wonders for morale and the successes will get bigger.

DON'T:

1. Leave till tomorrow what you could do today unless you need more time to consider the options; tomorrow may be too late.

2. Focus only on what you are good at from your past life; pick someone good to head up areas of your previous specializations and then get out of the way.

3. Underestimate the intelligence and the potential of your employees; they will amaze you if you let them.

4. Be too ready to make very visible changes if you are not absolutely sure that they will be consistent with the culture that you want to develop; reversing these later will appear as a failure for all to see and undermine your credibility and authority.

5. Try to be a CEO before you are ready; if you're fresh out of graduate school and have little management experience under your belt, you are unlikely to be ready.

6. Give up your life for this job; you will be a better CEO if you balance your professional and personal life, and remember that everyone, including you, is replaceable.

Chapter 2	**The Role of the CEO**

First, let it be said that your job as a CEO and head of the organization is the most fun of any in it but that with it goes tremendous responsibility. Your are an important link in the food chain of your employees, your suppliers, your customers, and the community at large. It is your duty to be good at what you do. This will require that you have sufficient experience and knowledge of the tools of the trade to adopt an holistic approach to the business so as to be able to capture and understand every facet of it and manage it professionally. The CEO is truly the integrating factor in the whole enterprise; the one who pulls everything together and makes it all work (or not, as the case may be).

The role of the CEO may be stated as follows using a travel analogy:

To provide the vision on where to go, to communicate clearly to everyone, including the company owners, the reason for travel, to describe the route in the form of a road map and timetable, to procure what will be needed for the journey, to select and mold the leadership team, to lead by example and provide cohesiveness and direction, to review progress against stated targets, thereby to get to the destination and at each stage of the journey successfully reached, to celebrate success.

The key ideas underlying this definition are: vision, communication, teambuilding, and leadership. This can be seen graphically in Chart 2.0.

In formulating our vision, we need to be clear about our destination, when we want to arrive, and to have a broad plan as to how we intend to get there. We shall consider this in much greater depth in the later chapter on "The Strategic Plan". We need to be able to communicate to everyone why we are going.

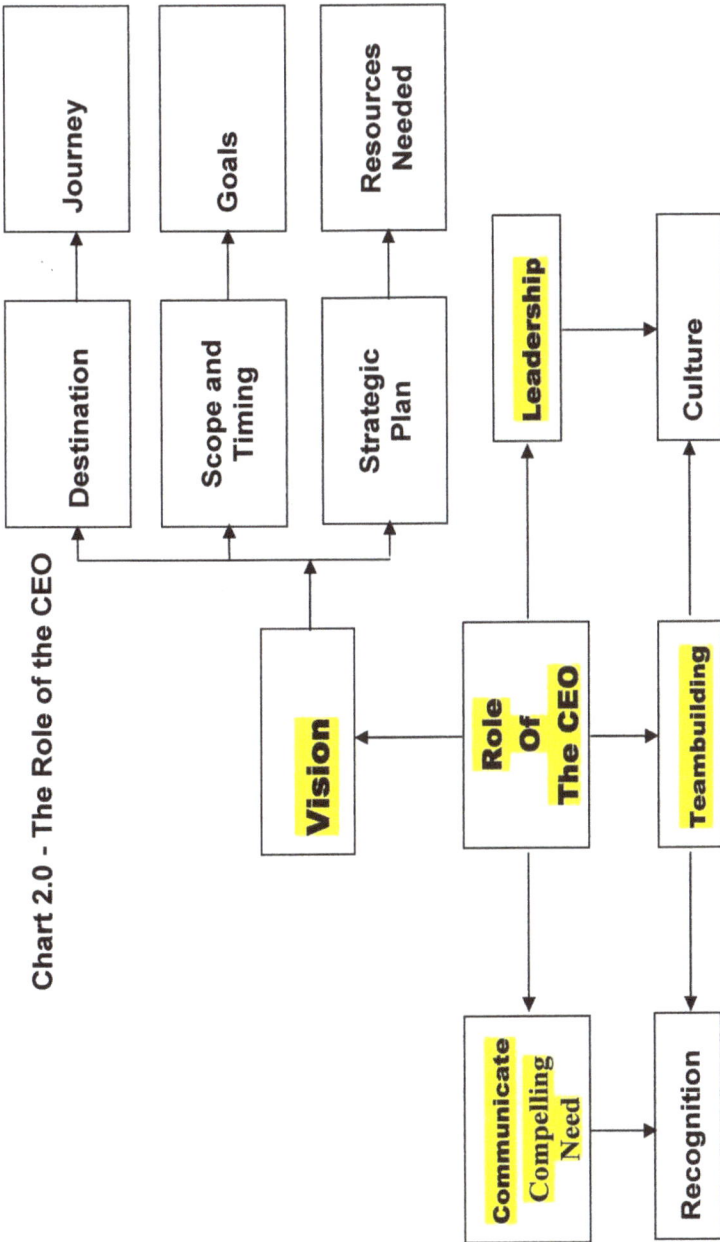

Chart 2.0 - The Role of the CEO

Journey

Goals

Resources Needed

Destination

Scope and Timing

Strategic Plan

Leadership

Culture

Vision

Role Of The CEO

Teambuilding

Communicate Compelling Need

Recognition

You should think of this as "**Communicating the Compelling Need**" for the journey and for change. For an organization that is losing market share rapidly to a more agile competitor, clearly the compelling need, as a minimum, is to stop the decline and to regain the company's former market position. Your workforce will readily understand this when it is communicated to them. For a company in trouble, the compelling need is usually fairly easy to state and to communicate. For a company that has done well historically but where significant change is required to ensure the company's future, the need for change will usually not be quite so straightforward to get across. This will be discussed in the later chapter "Communicating the Plan and the Compelling Need".

A Note on Priorities

In any organization, its leader is beset on a daily basis with a very large number of things that compete for their precious time. You will need to remain extremely focused if you are not to get distracted from the main task in hand. The following list contains the things that only you as CEO can address that will be developed in later chapters. Look at this list daily and check that you are allocating sufficient time to each area:

- Developing a Vision, Mission, Goals and Strategy and sticking to the task
- Focusing on the "Top Down" Priority Improvement Projects that will achieve the Goals (see later chapter on Goal Deployment)
- Reviewing progress at regular intervals on these projects
- Obtaining the necessary financial backing to get the job done
- Communicating upwards, downwards and sideways everything that you are trying to achieve
- Building the necessary team and people resources
- Making sure that everyone in the organization understands their role and what part they will play in the achievement of the Goals.
- Leading from the front and by example
- Creating an appropriate values and performance-based company Culture to succeed
- Celebrating success with Recognition Events

| Chapter 3 | The Strategic Plan |

Why do we need a Strategic Plan?

A Strategic Plan is basically a sales document whose main intent is usually one of the following:

For **External** Consumption:

- To persuade investors to give us funding

- To demonstrate to a third party that we know what we are doing and hence gain their confidence in us

- To persuade our Board of Directors, our parent company, and our boss to give us the resources that we need.

For **Internal** Consumption

- As an important intellectual process annually

- Formally to record our intentions

- To allow us "to keep score"

- As an important internal communication document.

What is a Strategic Plan?

A Strategic Plan is a clear statement of the organization's intentions and proposed actions over a stated timeframe.

It answers the **six questions** posed by Kotler (ref.1) that need to be answered. Kotler also identified the **six stages** in the strategic evaluation process.

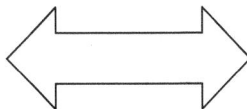

These are:

Question	Stage
1. Where are we now and why?	(Diagnosis)
2. Where are we going?	(Prognosis)
3. Where do we want to get to?	(Objectives)
4. How shall we get there?	(Strategy)
5. By what means shall we get there?	(Action Plan)
6. How shall we measure progress?	(Control)

You will find many books on strategic planning and the process to arrive at the appropriate strategy for a business. I shall simply share with you here the process that I used successfully as a strategic planner for three large international organizations, that I have since adapted after more than 25 years as a practicing CEO.

There are five key areas of analysis in arriving at a preferred strategic direction for your company:

- External Appraisal
- Internal Appraisal
- Strategic 0ptions Consideration
- Establishing a Vision, Mission and Goals
- Preparing the Strategic Plan

This is illustrated in Chart 3.0 and in more detail in Chart 3.1.

External Appraisal

In the External Appraisal, we consider everything <u>outside</u> of the firm. To do this we need to consider **environmental** factors.

These are normally listed as:
Legal / political, social / cultural, and economic.

A major change in any one of these environmental factors can create or kill a business. Lack of attention to these will, in the long run for sure in the short term probably, bring about your company's downfall. I cannot emphasize too strongly that you must make yourself aware of all the key trends in these environmental areas insofar as they relate to your business. Herein lies opportunity or death so be very thorough so as not to miss an important trend or event.

Chart 3.0
The Strategic Plan Evaluation Process in Brief

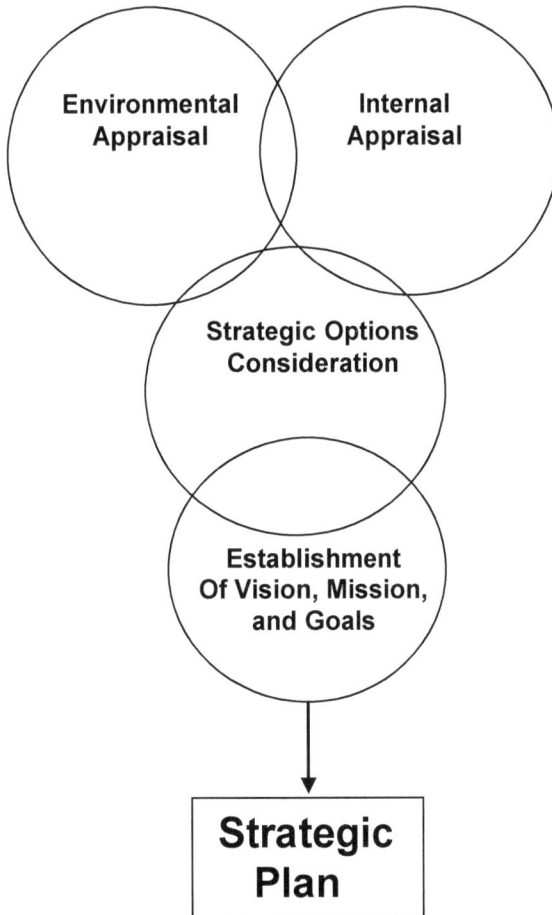

Environmental Appraisal

Internal Appraisal

Strategic Options Consideration

Establishment Of Vision, Mission, and Goals

Strategic Plan

Chart 3.1
The Strategic Planning Process
Inputs and Outputs

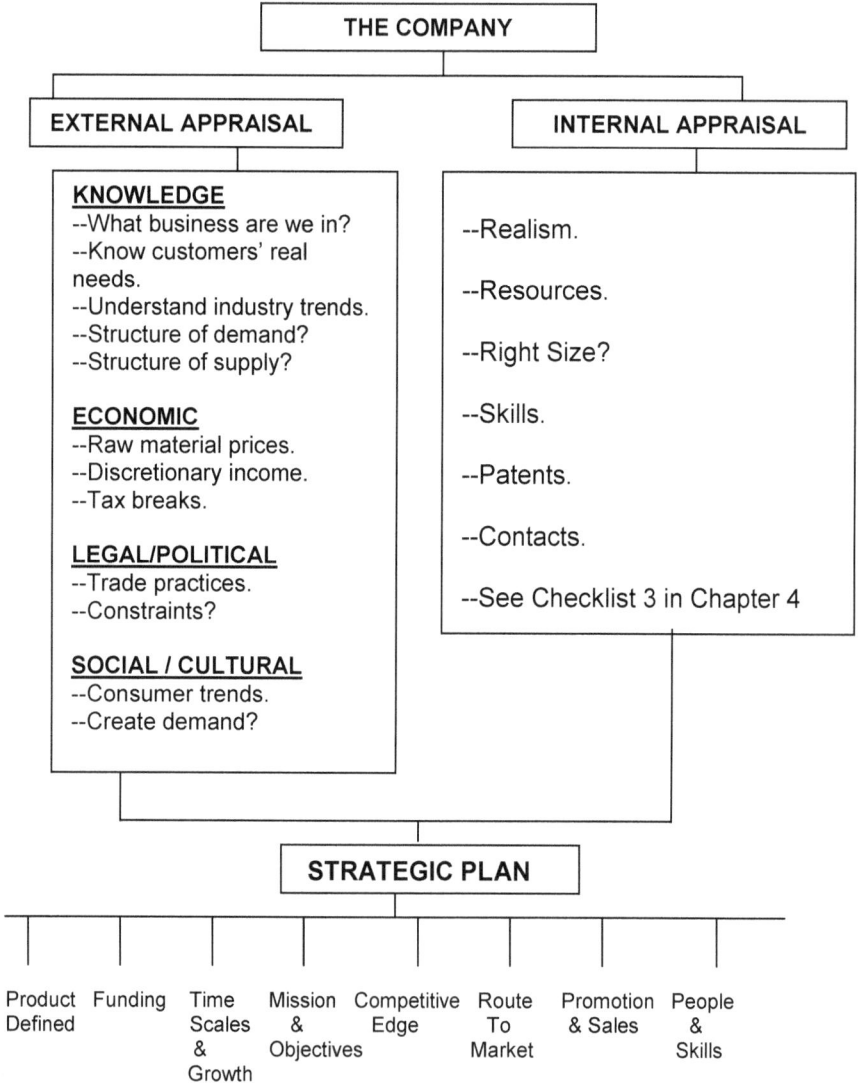

THE COMPANY

EXTERNAL APPRAISAL

INTERNAL APPRAISAL

KNOWLEDGE
--What business are we in?
--Know customers' real needs.
--Understand industry trends.
--Structure of demand?
--Structure of supply?

ECONOMIC
--Raw material prices.
--Discretionary income.
--Tax breaks.

LEGAL/POLITICAL
--Trade practices.
--Constraints?

SOCIAL / CULTURAL
--Consumer trends.
--Create demand?

--Realism.

--Resources.

--Right Size?

--Skills.

--Patents.

--Contacts.

--See Checklist 3 in Chapter 4

STRATEGIC PLAN

| Product Defined | Funding | Time Scales & Growth | Mission & Objectives | Competitive Edge | Route To Market | Promotion & Sales | People & Skills |

A good example of an environmental factor putting paid to a really fast growing business opportunity occurred to me while I was running one of the largest pari-mutuel gaming operations in the USA. My team and I had grown the business by over six times in five years. At the time, we were running four horse racetracks, a greyhound track, and six large teletheaters. A piece of legislation designed to control illegal use of gaming machines on native-American reservations in its interpretation by the federal district courts actually encouraged full casino gaming. It allowed the native-Americans to run casinos on our doorstep and gave us no right to compete on equal terms. This environmental factor brought about the demise of an important part of our business and threatened the rest. In this case, it was not so much of an oversight as a piece of badly enacted and interpreted legislation; but the result was the same.

It is the CEO's job to be fully abreast of these environmental factors and trends. This cannot be delegated. You can get people to help you gather information and stay in touch but in the end it is you who must have the information in your head. You will take the fall if you get it wrong so make it your business to get fully abreast early on and then stay appraised. One good way to do this is by being active in industry bodies if they exist in your industry. Get involved in some committee work. This has the added advantage that you will also get to meet and be able to measure the metal of some of your key competitors face to face.

Internal Appraisal

The next chapter "Internal Appraisal of the Company" deals with this in great detail.

Strategic Options Consideration

With all of the information that you have collected in the External and Internal Appraisals, you are now ready to review what options are open to your company in the future. This is best done by assembling your Company Leadership Team in a relaxed setting away from the offices and holding an "**awayday**". At this event, someone influential should act as **facilitator**, preferably someone who has considerable experience in strategic planning (see later chapter on Meetings Management). You may be well advised to bring someone in if your company does not have an

expert in this field. You will act as chairman of the proceedings and explain what the event is about, make decisions at appropriate moments, and call the group to order where necessary.

A good device to start the discussion is a **S**trengths, **W**eaknesses, **O**pportunities and **T**hreats (**SWOT)** analysis. This examines the strengths and weaknesses of your business and reviews the opportunities and threats that are foreseen. It ties together nicely the Internal and External Appraisals. The SWOT Analysis should be undertaken by the **company leadership team** at the awayday as the result of a **brainstorm.** In preparation for the awayday and the brainstorm, someone, preferably you, should write and circulate in advance papers on the Internal and External Appraisals. You should make it clear to each member of your leadership team that they should read and study the papers and come prepared to provide input to the **strategic options** debate at the awayday.

When you have completed the SWOT exercise with your leadership team, you will be in a good position to consider what strategic options are available to your company. The best tool for this is, once again, brainstorming. Here you should consider a number of background scenarios relating to the key environmental trends that affect your business, and arrive at a number of approaches to dealing with the opportunities offered and threats posed. Then you will prioritize the options and either arrive at a small number of preferred approaches for further evaluation and consideration or agree on **one preferred strategy**.

If it takes two meetings to get to the preferred strategy, then let it. In any event, the objective is to get the whole company leadership team behind one favored strategy. Once this group has agreed it, every member must become totally committed to it and to making it happen. At this point we are ready to develop our **Vision, Mission, and Goals**. This will be described in a later chapter.

There are just a few further pieces of advice. Firstly, approach this strategic options phase of the work as if you had no funding constraints, unless you are provided with guidelines from a corporate office that are different. If possible, answer the question "if we really unleashed this business, what could it

really achieve?" If you do have a parent, at some point in the process you are going to have to go back to them to get funding approval for your ambitious plan. However, corporate and your group CEO is going to look on you and your plan much more favorably if it is ambitious than if it is uninspired. If you don't have a parent, your board and your financial backers, whoever they may be, are also going to be much more excited by an ambitious plan.

Next, be careful not to get bogged down by "analysis paralysis". Try to get closure on the preferred strategy. You need to perform the background preparation described above. But you should also recognize that you will never have perfect information, and there comes a point when you just have to put a stop to requests for more information and go into the risk business, which is at the heart of business success. Judging this point is an important part of your role as CEO and an important opportunity for you to demonstrate leadership. So be bold and, above all, don't miss the big opportunity (or threat) for your business.

Lastly, you must create a collaborative mindset. Your facilitator should assist you with this. This is a fun exercise if managed well. It is a great opportunity for **teambuilding**. If you get significant disagreement from one or more members of your company leadership team to the preferred strategy, they are going to have to accept, as any member of a cabinet must, that they will adopt the cabinet's decision and throw their full weight behind it once the group has collectively agreed a course of action. If they feel unable to do this, their **only** recourse is to resign. You, too, must satisfy yourself that they are capable of and willing to pursue faithfully the collective decision. If you are not convinced of this, then you have no alternative but to remove them from the company leadership team. The business world is tough and you cannot afford to have a member of your leadership team not one hundred per cent with the group. It will waste much of your time down the road, dissipate the efforts of the group, and be a cause for much unrest and disharmony within it.

The Strategic Plan Structure

When all the analysis has been done and the preferred course of action decided, the Strategic Plan should be written up in the form of a document that can be used. This will record formally the intentions of The Leadership Team and act as a record against which progress can be measured.

The Structure of the document that should be produced is provided next in Checklist Number 2. Even after the preferred strategy has been arrived at there is clearly a lot of detail that needs to be filled in by individual departments and much forecasting and financial analysis.

References

1. Phillip Kotler, Marketing Management, 2nd Edition, Prentice Hall 1972.

Mentone, Alabama, in wintertime

Checklist Number 2 – The Strategic Plan Structure

1. **Executive Summary**
2. **Financial Projections and Funding Requirements**
3. **Mission, Objectives, and Goals**
4. **Environmental Appraisal**

   - Define and quantify the basic need
   - How will this be affected by economic, legal/legislative, social/cultural, & political trends
   - Demand forecasts for the business

5. **Competition Strategy**

   - What business are we really in; who/what is our competition?
   - What is our unique selling proposition (usp)?
   - How is our product better than the rest?
   - How should it be positioned in the marketplace?
   - What market share are we targeting?

6. **Marketing Plan**

   - Product strategy
   - Geographical focus and Distribution Strategy
   - Promotional Plan
   - Pricing Strategy by product

7. **Resource Plan**

   - Sources of finance
   - Detailed Cash Flow Projections
   - People needs
   - Facility requirements
   - Suppliers

8. **Objectives and Targets for the business**

   - Growth targets, sales volume, share penetration
   - Timing
   - Profit targets
   - Other targets…. going public, divestment, etc.

   - Mergers / acquisitions / disposals (see Ch. 23).

Chapter 4	Internal Appraisal of the Company

Checklist Number 3 provides a very useful roadmap for an Internal Appraisal of a company. Checklist Number 4 proposes typical remedies that might be considered. These checklists are especially useful when analyzing a company for the first time, for example when you have just joined a company. If we are to understand the business sufficiently well to organize our thoughts about what is important and get our priorities right, we need to go through a systematic series of questions. The experienced CEO will have this list pretty much in his head and will be able to cut to the chase quickly and instinctively to see where they need to spend their time. However, for those new to general management, it is a good idea to be really thorough and systematic at this stage so as not to miss something really important.

We shall now go through each of the questions in this checklist in turn and explain a little more fully what kind of analysis should be undertaken. Needless to say, the new CEO will require help with this work. In many cases there will be a chief financial officer or other members of the team who have much of the information already (if the team is any good). If not, then you are simply going to have to address the totality of this exercise over time and be prepared for it to take longer. Use those individuals who show an early willingness to assist you to get these analyses carried out.

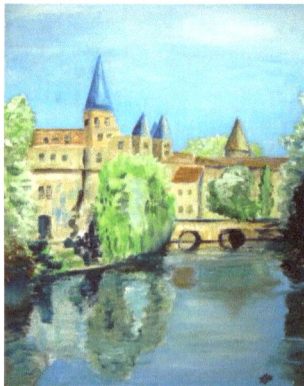

Oil Painting of French château by the author

Checklist Number 3 - Internal Appraisal of the Company

1. How successful are we financially / Where do we make money?
    - financial ratio analysis
    - product, market and customer profitability
    - Pareto (80/20 rule) analysis of sku s
    - value adding processes

2. How competitive are we?
    - raw material purchasing
    - labor rates

3. How efficient are we?
    - core business processes
    - process mapping
    - manpower productivity
    - yields and scrap
    - plant layout and logistics
    - inventory levels

4. What does our customer really value / how do we match up?
    - quality
    - price
    - delivery lead times
    - on-time delivery
    - order accuracy
    - support levels (customer service / technical)

5. How do we / should we measure our performance?
    - Metrics, relevant to our current situation
    - review frequency
    - corrective action process

6. How committed are our people?
    - level of employee empowerment
    - clear goals and objectives

7. How well do we use our scarce cash resources?
    - receivables and payables
    - inventory turns
    - cash forecasting
    - debt structure

Checklist Number 3 - Internal Appraisal of the Company (continued)

8.   How effective is our marketing and selling operation?
-    how effectively do we go to market?
-    size and quality of salesforce
-    journey planning
-    sales call structure
-    management of salesforce
-    remuneration and incentives

9.   What are our challenges in order of importance?
-    key factors for success
-    top ten things we must get right

10.   What is our Strategic Plan and how shall we achieve it?
-    actions arising from points 1-9 of diagnosis
-    growth - how big, how fast?
-    targets and metrics – how shall we measure progress?
-    goal deployment and improvement projects

Little River Canyon – Mentone, Alabama.

Checklist No. 4 -- Internal Appraisal Potential Remedies

Short Term

- Plant rationalization
- Productivity gains
- Process re-engineering
- Focus on value added activity
- Supply chain changes
- Product rationalization
- Restructured salesforce
- More efficient selling practices
- Greater customer focus
- Strengthening of the management team
- Improved forecasting
- Reduction in working capital
- Financial restructuring
- Greater use of measurement
- A results orientation
- Improved communication
- Streamlined systems
- Use of incentive programs
- Improved cash management
- Strong leadership and clearly defined company culture

Longer Term

- Joint venture
- Acquisition / Disposal
- New Product Development
- Total Quality Management (TQM)
- Total Productive Maintenance (TPM)
- Goal Deployment
- Lean Manufacturing

How successful are we financially?

You will, no doubt, have obtained some financial history for the company before you accept the job and will have a reasonable idea of how the company has faired in recent years. Now that you have joined the company, you should take the opportunity to get a lot more financial information, undertake some **financial ratio analysis**, and become completely familiar with trends in the financials and where the money is made and spent. You will need to look at **the income statement, balance sheet, and cash flow statement** for a number of years. These are the three key pieces of financial recording. Become familiar with the balance sheet and cash flow statements, what they mean, and how to use them. Businesses fail because they run out of cash, not necessarily because they are unprofitable.

If at all possible, you should try to get someone in finance to **benchmark** your company against a competitor (ideally the market leader) or a successful company operating in a very similar industry. This will be invaluable since it will allow you to judge how effective and efficient your company is relative to how it should and could be. Is your cost of sales to service a smaller market higher than the market leader, for example, and why? And so on. You can learn an enormous amount from these types of comparisons about the strengths and weaknesses of your company and how competitive are your products and services.

Where do we make money?

We need to ascertain which products, which customers, and which markets yield the highest gross margins and net profit. In order to do this, we have to make sure that our costs reflect the true cost of manufacture and distribution to our customer. Everything that is required to make and deliver the product and service the customer must be included. This is called **activity based costing**. You would be surprised to learn how few businesses really understand and answer the question of where they make money. You will also find some surprising results when you get the answer for your business. The reality never agrees completely with gut feel, intuition, and folklore. There are always products, customers and markets where everyone always believed that we made money. When the work is done we find, lo and behold, that we have been losing money there for

31

years; and the product, customer, or market, that we always suspected as being marginal, we suddenly find out is a bright star in our profitability firmament.

The second major area to look at is **product mix**. Your company will produce a large number of products and product variants. Each variant we shall call an sku. In most companies the number of skus increases over time simply because the sales department wants to satisfy every customer's needs and gets production to agree to create another product variant. The list gets longer because no-one thinks or bothers to cull old and unprofitable skus from the range, so they go on forever. To look at the product mix we prepare a **Pareto chart**. This plots sales volume as a percentage of the total on the ordinate or "y" axis and number of skus as a percentage of the total on the abscissa or "x" axis. It is almost always true that 20 per cent of your products account for more than 80 per cent of your sales volume. This was first observed by Mr. Pareto and so has become known as **"The Pareto Principle"**. It is otherwise known as the **"80/20 Rule"**. The important point to realize is that in most organizations that have been operating for any length of time there is a long "tail" involving many skus that have very low sales and contribute little to profitability. This is prime territory for profit improvement and we shall address this in a later chapter.

Lastly, we need to use a tool called **"process mapping"** to map the whole process from getting the order to receiving payment from the customer, with a view to identifying which parts of the process **add value** and which elements add little or no value. Those that add little or no value need to be eliminated, contracted out, or minimized in some way. You will be amazed at how many elements of the process currently performed by your organization really add no value. This is because organizations "evolve" and in many areas people do things the way they do simply because that seemed to be convenient or sensible at the time. Down the road, we end up doing the same things without regard to whether that is the best way or to whether it adds any value.

When you find out where you really make money, you can then begin to steer the business towards greater profitability.

Little River Canyon, Mentone, Alabama

How competitive are we?

You need to find out how you compare with your key enterprise competitors in five major areas of operation:

1. raw materials purchasing and efficiency of use of raw materials
2. labor rates
3. productivity
4. pricing
5. quality
6. lead times, delivery, and service.

This is not always easy to do. But you really need to know. If you pay more for your raw materials or have significantly lower yields and produce more scrap than your competitors, you will not survive long term. If you pay more for your labor in the area in which you operate and labor cost is a significant element in your cost builds up, you will not survive. This is especially true if you are in an international business and your competitors are overseas and they have access to significantly lower labor rates than you.

Your manufacturing or operational methodology needs to be the best it can be and at least as efficient as your competition, otherwise they will always be able to gain market share from you by offering lower prices, if price is a key customer decision criterion.

Your price competitiveness is relatively easy to establish. If you are forced to give bigger discounts than some of your

competitors, you are not truly competitive. Quality, lead times, delivery and service are a little more difficult to get at although your customers will normally be very happy to tell you exactly where you stand if you ask them.

This question of competitiveness demands some really thorough research. It is worth doing since it will influence greatly the strategy that you will select.

How efficient are we?

Related closely to the topic above is our efficiency. We have talked about yields and scrap and manpower productivity. This harks back to our business processes and whether they represent best practice. To achieve "best practice" requires that we have **benchmarked** organizations that really know what they are doing and have compared our operations with the world's best. Having done this, we have then followed up with pro-active management to bring our practices in line. If we have not yet done this, we need to do it pretty darn quickly and inject this into our strategy since no organization in today's world can survive for long if they are not efficient and striving to be the best. To become the best will require that every element of your operation conforms with the most modern operational philosophy. If we are a manufacturing operation, this means using **lean manufacturing** techniques (see later Chapter) including laying out the plant efficiently, achieving single-piece-flow and producing to customer requirement rather than for stock, using kaizen and continuous improvement to get steadily better, and working with suppliers to minimize inventories and receive raw materials just in time.

The other key requirement in business is that we are very efficient in our use of cash. Our invoicing and our cash collection need to be sharp. Inventory and work in process also need to be completely under management control and held at an absolute minimum.

What does our customer really value/ how do we measure up?

In any industry where enterprises compete for business there are a number of factors that affect the customer's decisions regarding the sourcing of goods or services. Your company may

have researched this and may already have a clear idea as to where the company needs to excel to beat off the competition. If they haven't, then you need to spend sufficient time with your customers to ascertain what it is that really turns them on and what they really value from you as a supplier. Ask them; for sure they will tell you in no uncertain terms.

The traditional motivators to a buyer are, of course, your product and its quality, price, delivery lead-time, on-time delivery, order accuracy, and support levels (customer service / technical). Research into many product categories shows that price is seldom the key decision maker since the buyer is normally trying to satisfy a complex equation of needs and is often prepared to pay more for quality, reliability, better service, etc.

When you know what it is that your customer is looking for, then you need to review objectively how you measure up against your competitors. This can be done scientifically for your product using a technique known as **quality function deployment** . For the other factors, the best way to arrive at your customer's real needs and to monitor regularly how you are doing is to strike a **customer-supplier agreement** and seek regular feed back from your customer as to how you are doing.

It goes without saying that if the results of this part of your initial diagnosis are not satisfactory you may have a really fundamental problem like not having a product that competes in the marketplace. Or you may have a gem of a product that has just never received the level of marketing support that it needs to get started. Either of these discoveries will clearly have a major impact on your strategy going forward.

How do we / should we measure our performance?

This is one of the commonest areas where companies are inadequate. Some companies measure just about everything and then do little with the information. Some measure virtually nothing. The trick is to decide what it is that you are setting out to do, where you want to see significant changes, and then to put in place measures that will allow you to monitor how you are doing on a regular basis. Only by doing this well will you exercise real control over your business. In addition, the **metrics** that you

measure will necessarily change over time as you make progress and your priorities alter.

Getting the right measures in place and being absolutely committed to reviewing these at carefully chosen and pre-determined intervals of time will go a long way to establishing a **results-oriented culture** within your organization. It is essential that you achieve this. A results-oriented culture requires that everyone knows what targets they as individuals and in groups are expected to achieve in their respective area of the business, and also that they understand what are the key targets that management are setting out to achieve for the business as a whole. The tool that you will use for this is **goal deployment** (see later chapter). Where the review process for the metrics identifies that targets are not being met, you will need to have in place a **corrective action process**. This will involve delegation of individual's and team's resources in a focused effort to get back on track.

To set targets, to delegate responsibility for action, to measure performance against the targets and to make any changes that may be necessary to redirect the business towards the achievement of its objectives is the absolute minimum that one can ask of management. Not to do this is dereliction of duty on the part of management.

How committed are our people?

You will get a measure of the commitment of your people simply by walking around and talking to people. You need to ascertain how empowered are your people, how motivated are they and do they have a clear sense of what is going on and how they may have an impact on it. If you have a workforce of disconnected and disenchanted people you have a goldmine to be tapped. These people are your key asset. Imagine the power for change if you could just get them working all together on the same goals and pulling in the same direction? What you are most likely to find is that you have a lot of highly motivated and well-intentioned people who are all pulling in opposite directions due to poor leadership. It is your job to provide just that direction and leadership.

How well do we use our scarce cash resources?

Cash is king. In general, businesses put far too much of their emphasis on profit (EBIT or EBITDA) performance. If you run out of cash and cannot make payroll, it doesn't matter how much profit you may be making because the game could be over. Note that not making payroll tax is a federal offence for which you as CEO are personally liable. We understand cashflow only too well with our own personal finances. It always comes down to choices. If we squander our cash on inefficient operations then we shall have insufficient funds to support the improvement and development of the business, and to do the positive things like market development and new product development that will create new opportunities and ensure survival.

You need to put in place cash forecasting and cash management. We shall develop this in a later chapter. However, as part of your initial diagnosis, you should look at how efficiently your business turns over its inventory and whether there is an opportunity to work with your suppliers to reduce your inventory by making them either hold inventory for you or manufacture just in time and supply you as your need arises. You should evaluate whether you should produce to order or whether for stock. It is much better to produce to order if possible, but this requires your manufacturing processes to be much more efficient if you are to be able to offer short lead times. You should look at how effectively you turn your receivables into cash from your customers and whether there is any opportunity to shorten your payment terms with your customer. This will result in a one time cash inflow. Likewise, there may be an opportunity to extend your payment terms with your suppliers also to achieve a cash inflow. **In short, cash needs to be managed.**

Are you lumbered with too much debt? Can you restructure your finances so as to relieve the burden of debt? These are things that you will need to come to terms with and may become important items on your radar screen of priorities.

How effective is our marketing and selling operation?

The key question here is "how effectively do we go to market?". We need to understand the level of marketing effort that is applied in terms of money and resources and how effective this

is. Do we use a traditional sales force or some other selling vehicle such as the Internet or telephone selling? Are these appropriate in the 21st Century? How much do we spend on advertising and promotional activity and is this money well spent? Does anybody really know (i.e. is the effectiveness actually measured)?

You have no doubt inherited a sales force. You need to spend as much time with these folk as you can early on both individually and as a group because between them they probably know more about what is going on out there in the marketplace than anyone. You will hear their pet theories and gripes; but you will also get a tremendous amount of insight. They will also know first hand how competitive are your products and how well positioned are they relative to the competition.

Furthermore, selling is something of a science these days. Good salesmen need a lot of training and managing. If you yourself have never been in sales and trained by a top notch, world class sales trainer, you may wish to take some external advice and get a professional sales trainer to undertake an audit to ascertain just how good your sales people are and to implement a training program for the whole sales force and marketing management.

The two last sections on Checklist #3 **"What are our challenges in order of importance?"** and "**How shall we achieve our strategic plan?**" will be dealt with in the next chapters.

Mountain Stream in Mentone, Alabama

| Chapter 5 | Defining the Vision, Mission, and Goals |

The **Vision Statement** describes in the simplest terms the very essence of what a company is all about and why it should exist. To do this in just a few words is not easy at all and requires considerable insight and wordsmithing skills. The shorter the Vision Statement the better, and the more likely it is that people in your organization (yourself included) will be able to memorize it and be able to repeat it. To be of value, it must be memorized by all and stated at the beginning of every meeting. As the key leader in the organization, the CEO should draft the Vision Statement with his **leadership team**. If he inherits a pre-existing Vision Statement, he must take ownership of it or scrap it and start afresh. Personally, I never came across one that I did not change! They are usually much too fluffy and vague.

The **Mission Statement** describes again briefly what has to be done for the Vision to be achieved. This will include statements about, among other things, customers, products, markets, quality, customer service, and financial performance.

The **Goals** address specific areas of management activity and state in simple terms what has to be achieved in order for the Mission to be accomplished and the Vision to become a reality.

Example

A real example is from a U.K. bathroom shower manufacturer that I ran and sold showers throughout the world. Note that the Vision Statement might seem a bit grandiose, but this company was externally accredited to be a world class company and won a prestigious award in the UK as "The Best UK Engineering Factory".

Vision: "To be the best quality, lowest cost producer of showers in the world."

Mission: "We shall increase customer preference for our brands by exceeding their expectations with superior quality products and services.

We shall achieve this through the involvement of all our people and business partners in the continuous improvement of our products, processes, and facilities; thereby sustaining superior financial performance."

Goals:

1. Grow relative market share through improved customer satisfaction whilst maintaining price premium.
2. Design and supply defect free product.
3. Involve all our people in the continuous improvement of our business.
4. Simplify the business by focusing on core processes and driving out waste.
5. Improve the contribution and performance of our suppliers.

This set of Vision, Mission, and Goals will be referred to again in a later chapter when we shall see how we use it in **Goal Deployment**.

How to Perform a Team Purpose Analysis

Whenever I join a new organization, I always do one very important exercise with the **leadership team**. I assemble my initial management team, preferably off-site, and we perform a specific **brainstorm** exercise. The most valuable tool for establishing our Vision, Mission and Goals is the **team purpose analysis**. This tool can be used in any situation where a group of people are gathered together in any organization or human enterprise. It is just as relevant in trade committees, parent teacher associations, charities, etc. as it is in the boardroom. It is essential for the CEO to be familiar with this technique. Ideally, they should facilitate the process themself, but, if they are not comfortable with this, they should select a very able facilitator to lead the group through the process.

The Team Purpose Analysis identifies what we want to be as an enterprise. The result is expressed as statements of Vision, Mission, and Goals.

It uses an organized and **facilitated brainstorming process** around the following areas:

- **Target market(s)**
  1. **Geographic focus**
  2. **Key customers**
- **Size, aspirations, and timescale**
- **Customer needs and the opportunity**
- **Specific services to be offered**
- **Management style**
- **Core values**
- **Culture**
- **Experience and skill sets of the Team members**
- **Competitive advantages.**
- **Challenges facing the industry and our organization**

Basically what the **facilitator** does is to ask the members of the group to provide ideas in a free flow format about what the organization is setting out to be and do and why it exists at all. All ideas must be captured without comment from others in the group except requests for clarification, this being the key rule in brainstorming. The simplest method of capture is to write the essence of the idea onto 3M stickers and to stick these to a wall. When all ideas have been presented, they are organized into common themes under common headings e.g. customers, markets, facilities, employees, etc. Normally, about six to ten themes are manageable.

These six to ten themes may then be prioritized for perceived level of importance to the group using a simple voting technique (i.e. giving each participant a few votes and asking each to ascribe votes to the key themes identified). In the same way, items within themes should be prioritized.

This analysis by the group then provides the essential material against which a **Vision Statement** can be crafted. At this stage, it is helpful for the group to stand back and reflect and then get each member to come up with a simple sentence in the form of a Vision Statement, one that captures the very essence of what the group is about. By selecting the preferred statement and the whole group then working to improve on the wording, it is possible to come up with a crisp and economic description for the **Vision**. It is likewise then possible to do the same thing for

the **Mission Statement** and the **Goals**. The whole process can be completed in about one hour with experienced facilitation. This may be the most efficient and effective use of one hour's time that the group will ever experience and is well worth the investment. Involving the whole board or executive leadership team achieves buy-in from the outset.

What are our challenges in order of importance?

From this session, we now have our **Vision, Mission, and Goals**. At this session, we can also identify the key projects that the company needs to address to achieve its goals. In this way we can arrive at what will be referred to as the ten "**Top Down Priority Improvements Projects**" or "**Cross Functional Improvement Projects**". Note that ten is the maximum number that you should attempt to tackle with your management team initially. The list is always longer but you must be single-minded about restricting the number of challenges that you take on at any one time. **Focusing on the priority issues is one of the keys to successful leadership**.

Do not discard the rejected projects. Keep them on a separate list because you will get back to them when you have made progress with the other top ten. It is important that you communicate to the rest of your management not only the top ten projects but also the list of items that will not be tackled yet. If you do not do this, some of your people may be tempted to stray into the non-priority issues and waste valuable time working on non-priority projects. You should also tell your boss and your board which items will not be tackled yet so that they do not keep asking you for a progress report in these areas. In this way, you will manage their expectations, buy yourself time, and stay in control of your own and the company's destiny and not get distracted or blown off course.

At every subsequent meeting when the leadership team gets together, these priority "Top Down Projects" should be reviewed briefly but thoroughly for progress. It helps to have a single chart that shows the issues, the champion (see later chapter on "**Project Management**"), the actions being taken and a date when the action will be completed. I prefer a "traffic light" system that indicates against each key action whether we are ahead, on, or behind schedule using green, amber and red markers. In this way one can see at a glance where we are falling behind and

thus where corrective action and intervention (by you) needs to occur.

| **Chapter 6** | How do we make the Strategic Plan Happen? |

Whether you can make the Strategic Plan happen or not is what sorts out the men from the boys. This is where the rubber hits the road!

The answer to the question "How do we make the Strategic Plan happen?" is the same as the answer to the question "How do you eat an elephant?". The answer is, of course, "One bite at a time"! We need to break the Strategic Plan down into bite-sized chunks and then assign each to individuals with responsibility and accountability for making it happen.

So far we have a Vision, Mission, Company Goals, and ten "Top Down Priority Improvement Projects" for the company as a whole. The company goals need to be broken down by department and by individual. The goals will then all have improvement projects associated with them for the company as a whole, for departments, and for individuals. The best way to illustrate this is with the Total Quality Management (TQM) Roadmap that I developed some years ago.

First of all, a note on Total Quality Management.

What is Total Quality Management?

Total Quality Management (TQM) involves a number of basic concepts:

1. Knowing exactly what the customer wants and making sure they get it
2. **Continuous Improvement** is a necessity not a choice
3. The person operating the machine or doing the job knows more about that operation than anyone else
4. Therefore, to get continuous improvement of all processes you must involve all employees
5. So, train them appropriately and provide them with the necessary skills and resources
6. Push as much responsibility down to the workplace as they can sensibly handle
7. Reward and recognize genuine improvement activity.

The Total Quality Management Roadmap

It is very important from the outset to take an holistic approach. The roadmap in Chart 6.0 that will be presented here involves a total Quality Management approach.

Chart 6.0

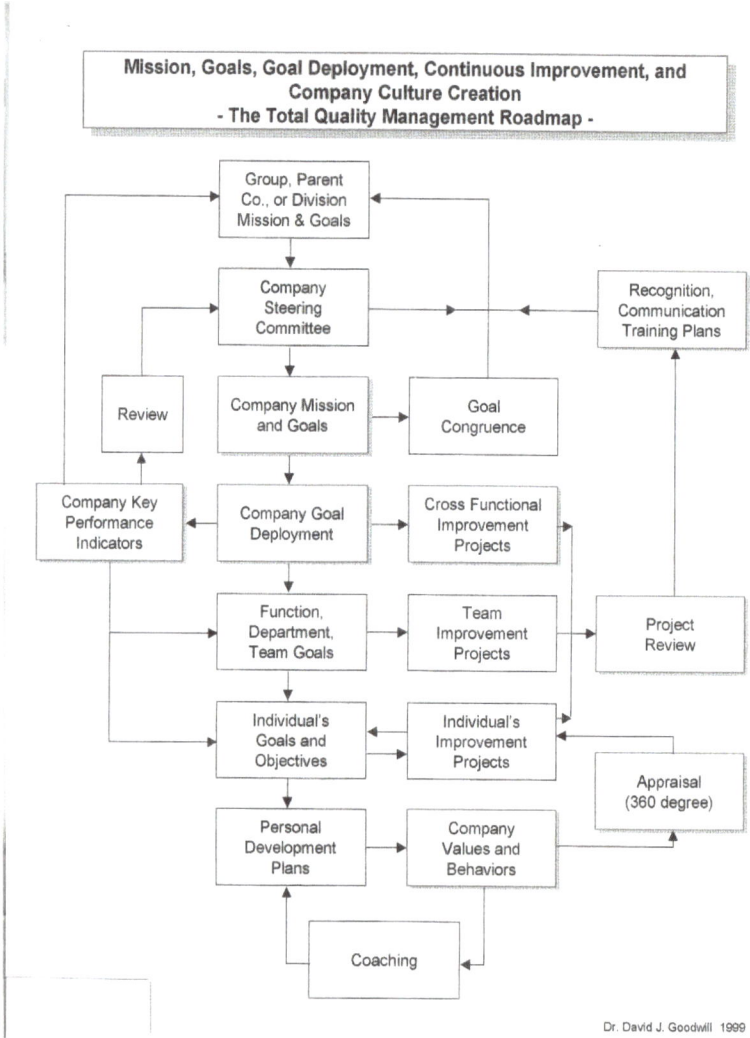

Dr. David J. Goodwill 1999

I have arrived at this roadmap after many years of successfully delivering Strategic Plan results and as a keen advocate of TQM. The reason that I would recommend it is that it contains three of the key CEO tasks namely:

- Goal Deployment
- Continuous Improvement Through Project Focus
- Creating a Values-Based Corporate Culture.

I shall return to each of these in much more depth in later chapters. All that I am trying to achieve at this stage is a very broad overview of what it is that we shall be setting out to put in place. The rest of this chapter will walk us through Chart 6.0, so follow the chart.

So, if we start at the top of Chart 6.0, and assume that your company is a subsidiary or division of a larger entity, there will probably be a group or divisional mission and goals that your organization will need to recognize and be party to. You will need to gain a clear understanding of these from the outset. To do this, spend time with your Chairman or with the people that recruited you. It is most important that you understand what they expect of you and how your performance will be measured.

During the Strategic Planning process, you will already have established your "**Company Leadership Team**". On Chart 6.0 this is referred to as the "**Company Steering Committee**", which is simply TQM terminology and is the same thing. This could be your board, executive or operating committee, or a special committee formed of appropriate leadership team players for the specific purpose of overseeing this operational roadmap and providing operational direction to the business. Using the technique described in the last chapter, the Team has developed the **Mission and Goals Statement** for your company; one that is entirely consistent with the group or divisional mission and goals. If you do not have group or divisional mission and goals statements to conform to, then you may be less constrained in the development of these for your company.

These goals will be broken down throughout the company in a process known as **Goal Deployment,** which will be described in detail in the next chapter. At the end of this process, everyone in the company will know what are their individual priorities and objectives and how these fit in with the company goals. The

method that will be used to achieve company, department, and individual's goals and targets will be through effective **Project Management**. This is the subject of a later chapter. These projects will involve the whole company for the ten "**Top Down Priority Improvement Projects**" or "**Cross Functional Improvement Projects**", individual departments and teams, and also individuals. In the case of the "Top Down Priority Improvement Projects" or "Cross Functional Improvement Projects" this will involve teams of specialists selected from each function across the whole or part of the organization.

The idea of using projects and teams to achieve goals will be developed in detail in the chapter on **Project Management**. Every project will need to be reviewed on a regular basis, and successes communicated back to the workforce and celebrated with due acclaim as part of a carefully coordinated **Recognition** program to be described in a later chapter. In this way, the organization will know how well the company is doing and will develop a keen sense of the progress that is being made. In time, the organization will enjoy the confirmation that recognition brings, will become hungry for success, and will relish every breakthrough and goal achieved. The Company Leadership Team will play a major part in reviewing the key projects and in organizing communication and recognition events at regular intervals. Company-wide training programs should also be closely aligned to the company's needs as identified through the Goal Deployment Process, and, based on this, the Company Leadership Team should specify training needs.

At the same time as arriving at the company goals, it is essential to identify the measures and metrics that will be used to monitor progress towards achieving these goals. These we shall call the "**Key Performance Indicators**". The method for selecting and adopting the right measures will be described in a later chapter.

In order for the company to **Create a Values-based Corporate Culture** that you as CEO want, the Leadership Team under your close guidance will specify the **Values** that it wishes to espouse. **Behaviors** can then be associated with these values. Now, behavior may be measured and changed or adapted over time. The driving force for these changes will be the **Appraisal Process**, which should focus on these selected behaviors. Each individual's performance should be assessed at regular intervals

against these behaviors. Programs to improve an individual's performance may then be put in place in the form of a **Personal Development Plan (PDP)**. To assist with the achievement of the PDP, a **coach** should be nominated to work with the individual. In this way, by gradually adapting the behavior of all individuals within the company to reflect the espoused **Values** of the company, a clear-cut culture will develop over time. This values-driven process for creating company culture will be explained in detail in a later chapter.

Chart 6.0 then will become your operational roadmap. At this stage you simply need to understand it and have an overall appreciation of what is contained within it.

East Brow of Lookout Mountain, Mentone, Alabama

Chapter 7	Goal Deployment

In the last section, we learned the importance of Goal Deployment to the achievement of the Strategic Plan. In the **Total Quality Roadmap**, we saw how the whole process fits together. Chart 7.0 focuses on the part of the chart that deals with **Goal Deployment.**

We have described how the company should arrive at the **Mission and Goals** in an earlier Chapter. The **Company Leadership Team** ("Company Steering Committee") should confirm that these are congruent with the Board's or Group's Goals, if there exists this higher authority.

These company goals need then to be broken down into individual function and departmental goals. This process is achieved firstly by identifying the ten "**Top Down Priority Improvement Projects**" that the company needs to address to achieve the **Company Goals**. These should number about ten to avoid overload and loss of focus. To each of these "Top Down Priority Improvement Projects" is allotted a **Sponsor,** who is a member of the Company Leadership Team ("Company Steering Committee") and is the most suitable individual to sponsor that particular project. A real example of this is illustrated in Chart 7.1. This is the same shower company for which we showed the development of a **Vision, Mission, and Goals** in a previous Chapter.

The Sponsor will be responsible for the management of that project and for making sure that the project receives the appropriate resources from across the company. He should therefore be a senior individual and should be a direct report of the CEO. This will be dealt with in a later chapter on **Project Management**. For projects that require an holistic approach and involve many departments, the CEO should sponsor the project himself. No Leadership Team Member, including the CEO, should sponsor more than three projects because this is a very time consuming role and is in addition to the Leadership Team Member's functional and departmental responsibilities.

Chart 7.0	**Goal Deployment**

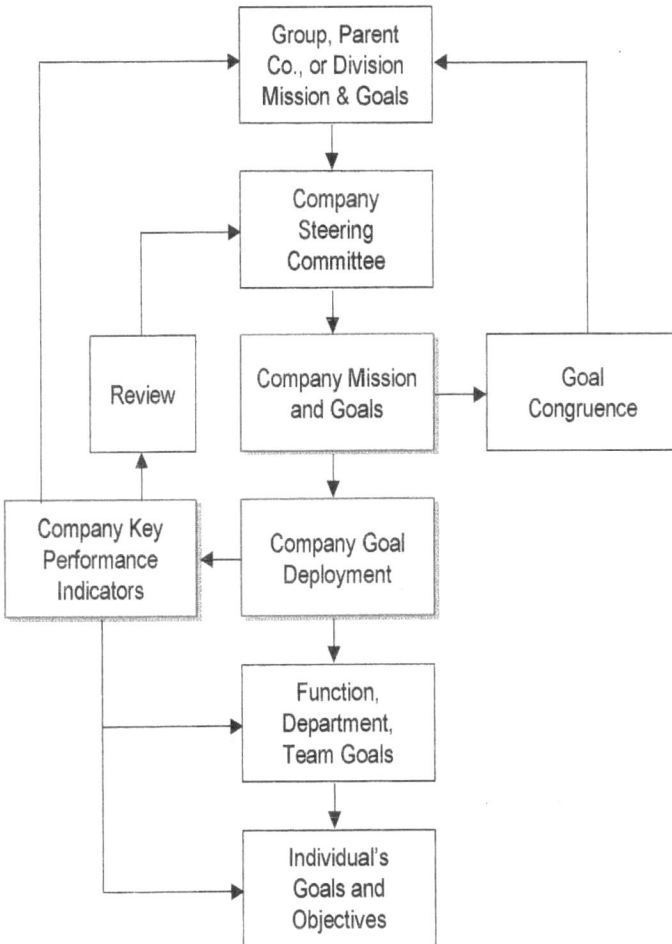

```
                    ┌─────────────────┐
              ┌────→│  Group, Parent  │←──────┐
              │     │ Co., or Division │       │
              │     │  Mission & Goals │       │
              │     └────────┬────────┘       │
              │              ↓                 │
              │     ┌─────────────────┐        │
              │   ┌→│    Company      │        │
              │   │ │    Steering     │        │
              │   │ │   Committee     │        │
              │   │ └────────┬────────┘        │
              │   │          ↓                 │
     ┌────────┤ ┌───────┐ ┌──────────────┐ ┌──────────┐
     │        │ │       │ │Company Mission│ │   Goal   │
     │        │ │Review │←│   and Goals   │→│Congruence│
     │        │ │       │ └──────┬───────┘ └──────────┘
     │        │ └───▲───┘        ↓
     │  ┌─────────────────┐ ┌──────────────┐
     │  │  Company Key    │ │ Company Goal │
     │  │  Performance    │←│  Deployment  │
     │  │  Indicators     │ └──────┬───────┘
     │  └────────┬────────┘        ↓
     │           │        ┌──────────────┐
     │           └───────→│   Function,  │
     │                    │  Department, │
     │                    │  Team Goals  │
     │                    └──────┬───────┘
     │                           ↓
     │                    ┌──────────────┐
     └───────────────────→│ Individual's │
                          │  Goals and   │
                          │  Objectives  │
                          └──────────────┘
```

Goodwill: The Chief Executive's Survival Kit

Chart 7.1 An Example of Goal Deployment "Top Down Projects"

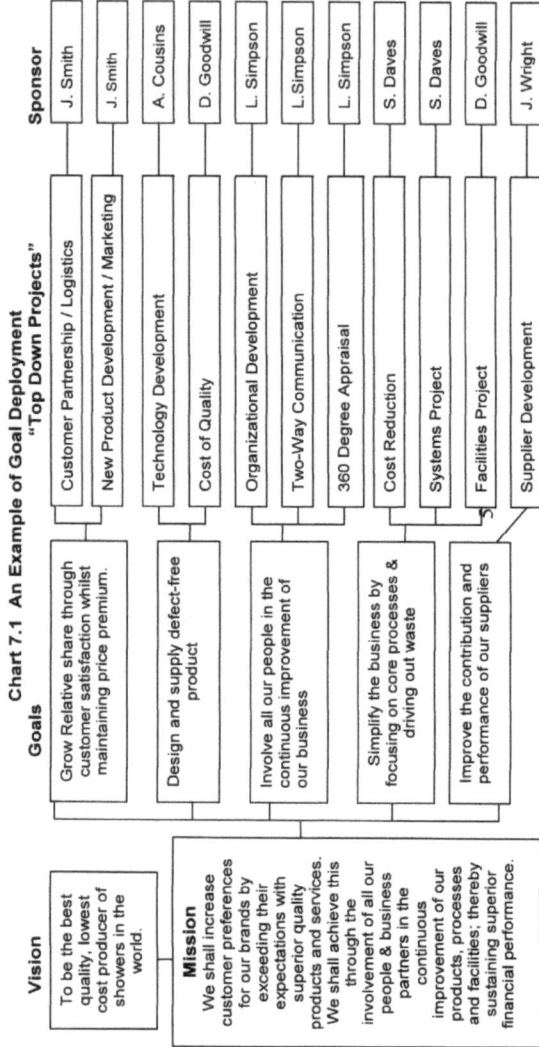

Vision

To be the best quality, lowest cost producer of showers in the world.

Mission

We shall increase customer preferences for our brands by exceeding their expectations with superior quality products and services. We shall achieve this through the involvement of all our people & business partners in the continuous improvement of our products, processes and facilities; thereby sustaining superior financial performance.

Goals

- Grow Relative share through customer satisfaction whilst maintaining price premium.
- Design and supply defect-free product
- Involve all our people in the continuous improvement of our business
- Simplify the business by focusing on core processes & driving out waste
- Improve the contribution and performance of our suppliers

Top Down Projects	Sponsor
Customer Partnership / Logistics	J. Smith
New Product Development / Marketing	J. Smith
Technology Development	A. Cousins
Cost of Quality	D. Goodwill
Organizational Development	L. Simpson
Two-Way Communication	L. Simpson
360 Degree Appraisal	L. Simpson
Cost Reduction	S. Daves
Systems Project	S. Daves
Facilities Project	D. Goodwill
Supplier Development	J. Wright

The Sponsor will then gather the appropriate functional individuals required to address the project and set goals for those functions and departments together with the functional and departmental heads. These **Functional and Departmental Goals** will then be used to set **Individual's Goals and Objectives** throughout the organization. Chart 7.0 illustrated this process. Chart 7.2 illustrates Goal Deployment for the Technical Function in a real life situation. All the projects on the right hand side will be allotted to individuals within the technical function.

This all sounds a little complex but it really isn't. It requires organization and a Leadership Team committed to doing the job properly. It also requires "give and take" when it comes to a functional director allotting his or her resources to another Project Sponsor for the good of the company. The functional director is normally a sponsor of one or more projects themself, so they know the score. But there is no place here for empire builders!

Another snowy Mentone, Alabama, day.

Chart 7.2 Technical Function Goal Deployment

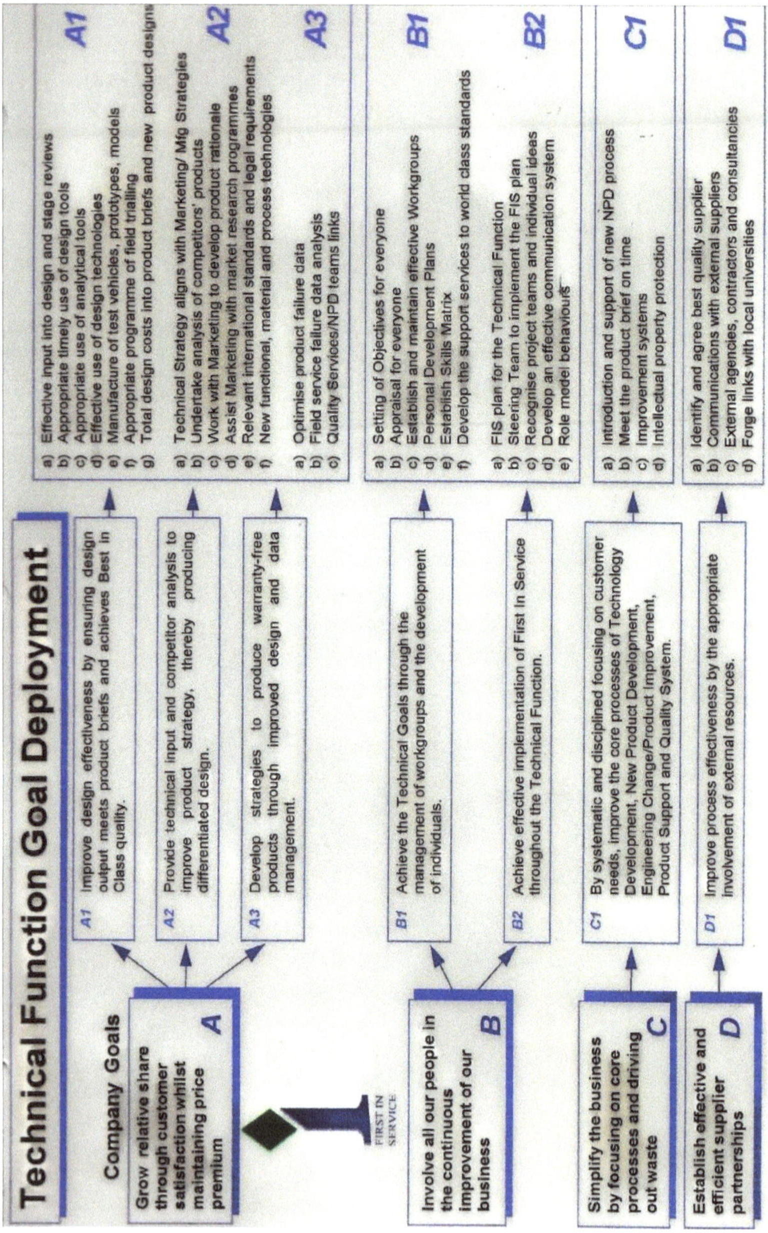
Technical Function Goal Deployment
Company Goals
Grow relative share through customer satisfaction whilst maintaining price premium
A
FIRST IN SERVICE
Involve all our people in the continuous improvement of our business
B
Simplify the business by focusing on core processes and driving out waste
C
Establish effective and efficient supplier partnerships
D
A1 Improve design effectiveness by ensuring design output meets product briefs and achieves Best in Class quality.
A2 Provide technical input and competitor analysis to improve product strategy, thereby producing differentiated design.
A3 Develop strategies to produce warranty-free products through improved design and data management.
B1 Achieve the Technical Goals through the management of workgroups and the development of individuals.
B2 Achieve effective implementation of First In Service throughout the Technical Function.
C1 By systematic and disciplined focusing on customer needs, improve the core processes of Technology Development, New Product Development, Engineering Change/Product Improvement, Product Support and Quality System.
D1 Improve process effectiveness by the appropriate involvement of external resources.
a) Effective input into design and stage reviews
b) Appropriate timely use of design tools
c) Appropriate use of analytical tools
d) Effective use of design technologies
e) Manufacture of test vehicles, prototypes, models
f) Appropriate programme of field trialling
g) Total design costs into product briefs and new product designs
A1
a) Technical Strategy aligns with Marketing/ Mfg Strategies
b) Undertake analysis of competitors' products
c) Work with Marketing to develop product rationale
d) Assist Marketing with market research programmes
e) Relevant international standards and legal requirements
f) New functional, material and process technologies
A2
a) Optimise product failure data
b) Field service failure data analysis
c) Quality Services/NPD teams links
A3
a) Setting of Objectives for everyone
b) Appraisal for everyone
c) Establish and maintain effective Workgroups
d) Personal Development Plans
e) Establish Skills Matrix
f) Develop the support services to world class standards
B1
a) FIS plan for the Technical Function
b) Steering Team to implement the FIS plan
c) Recognise project teams and individual ideas
d) Develop an effective communication system
e) Role model behaviours
B2
a) Introduction and support of new NPD process
b) Meet the product brief on time
c) Improvement systems
d) Intellectual property protection
C1
a) Identify and agree best quality supplier
b) Communications with external suppliers
c) External agencies, contractors and consultancies
d) Forge links with local universities
D1

| Chapter 8 | Continuous Improvement – Project Focus |

In the last section we reviewed how through the **Goal Deployment** process, **Company Goals** were broken down into **Function and Department Goals**. These were then broken down into **Individual's Goals and Objectives**. The last chapter and Chart 8.0 shows how these then become projects at the company, department and individual levels.

It is worth just saying a few words about how important are **projects** towards achieving a company's Goals. We manage the whole process through projects. **Project Management** therefore must be a core skill since it provides the vehicle to maintain control of the whole **Continuous Improvement** process. Project Management will be discussed in detail in the next chapter.

As was discussed in a previous chapter, one of the core concepts of Total Quality Management is that everyone should strive to get better and to improve all the processes within their control from top to bottom in the company. This continuous improvement happens by setting targets at every level of the organization, by training everyone in the company how to improve their work situation through the use of TQM techniques, getting them to define their improvement projects, and then giving them the resources to get the job done. This project focus is organized, disciplined, allows progress to be reviewed regularly, and requires that the use of company's limited resources be carefully monitored and controlled.

...one of the core concepts of Total Quality Management is that everyone should strive to get better and to improve all the processes....

| Chart 8.0 | **Continuous Improvement Through Project Focus** |

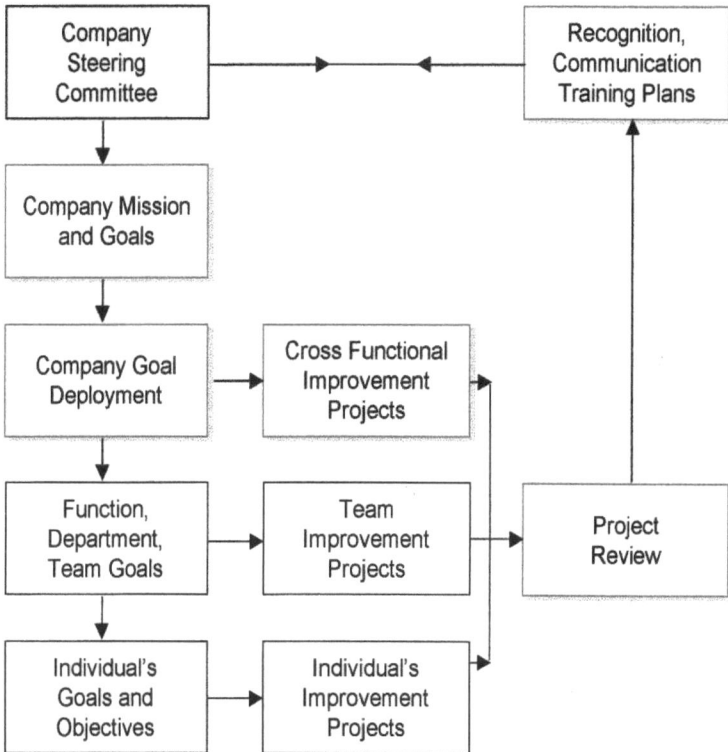

```
┌──────────────┐                              ┌──────────────┐
│   Company    │                              │ Recognition, │
│   Steering   │ ──────►        ◄───────────  │Communication │
│  Committee   │                              │Training Plans│
└──────┬───────┘                              └──────────────┘
       │                                              ▲
       ▼                                              │
┌──────────────┐                                      │
│Company Mission│                                     │
│  and Goals   │                                      │
└──────┬───────┘                                      │
       │                                              │
       ▼                                              │
┌──────────────┐     ┌──────────────┐                 │
│Company Goal  │     │Cross Functional│               │
│ Deployment   │ ──► │ Improvement  │ ───┐            │
│              │     │  Projects    │    │            │
└──────┬───────┘     └──────────────┘    │            │
       │                                  ▼            │
       ▼                             ┌──────────────┐  │
┌──────────────┐  ┌──────────────┐   │              │  │
│  Function,   │  │    Team      │   │   Project    │  │
│ Department,  │─►│ Improvement  │──►│   Review     │──┘
│ Team Goals   │  │  Projects    │   │              │
└──────┬───────┘  └──────────────┘   └──────────────┘
       │                                  ▲
       ▼                                  │
┌──────────────┐  ┌──────────────┐        │
│ Individual's │  │ Individual's │        │
│  Goals and   │─►│ Improvement  │────────┘
│  Objectives  │  │  Projects    │
└──────────────┘  └──────────────┘
```

| Chapter 9 | **Project Management** |

We have seen how Continuous Improvement in companies is achieved through good Project Management. Good Project Management occurs through good organization. This means the right people with the right tools and the right resources. Chart 9.0 shows a world class project management structure.

We have already seen how we should focus on the ten **"Top Down" Priority Improvement Projects**, these being selected for their potential impact on the company's results. A project management professional should be nominated as **Head of Projects**. Their role should be to oversee the process of **Project Management** and to supervise the team of **Project Managers**. As already discussed, each project should have a **Sponsor** from the **Leadership Team,** whose role is to oversee the project and make sure that the team has the resources it needs and makes the necessary progress.

As well as a Project Manager, each project should have a **Team Leader** and a **Team**. These individuals will be seconded from individual functions and may have to work full-time on the project. For their project, they report directly to the Project Manager (not their functional boss, note) and, through the Project Manager, to the Project Sponsor. To avoid conflict, the Project Sponsors will work out time allocation for individuals seconded to project teams with the **Functional Directors**, who will be their colleagues on the Company's Leadership Team, and will also have projects that they sponsor. This is all shown schematically in Chart 9.0. It works well given a Leadership Team committed to Continuous Improvement through Project Management.

The CEO should chair a **Project Review Meeting** regularly (normally weekly) which the Head of Projects and Sponsors should attend. Individual Project Managers and Team Members may be invited to present as required. At this meeting, any time conflicts or changes in priorities can be discussed and agreed.

Goodwill: The Chief Executive's Survival Kit

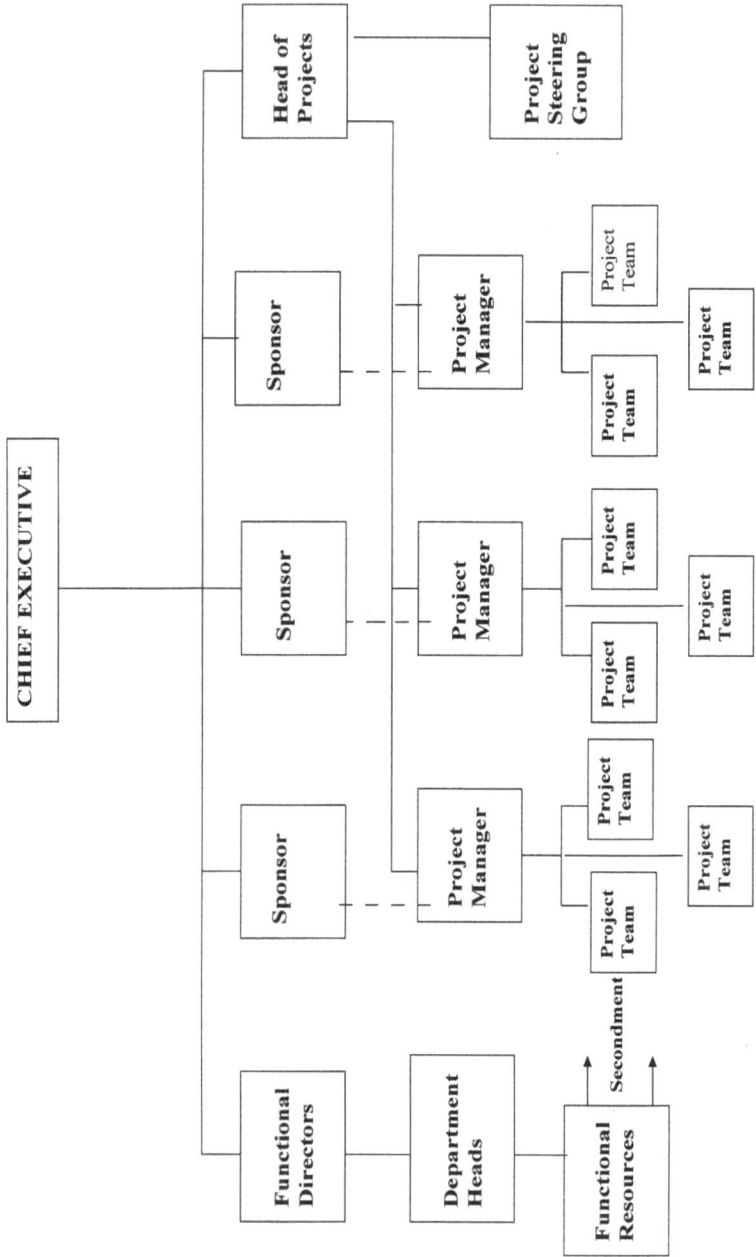

CHART 9.1   PROJECT MANAGEMENT – ORGANIZATION

57

A **Project Room** should be set aside specifically for Project Management, where the project teams can meet and leave their Gantt Charts displayed on the walls. In this way, interested parties can assess each project's progress at a glance.

Significant project accomplishments should be celebrated at **Recognition Events** that should be planned to occur at least monthly. A later Chapter will deal with this important motivational aspect.

The "London Eye", London, England

| Chapter 10 | How To Create a Values-based Corporate Culture |

Introduction

One of the key challenges for the leader of any organization is to create a consistent and recognizable culture. This is part of the very essence of their role and does not happen overnight. Leaders in the past have often done this simply with the force of their personality. This approach can be inconsistent, is very hard to communicate to the organization, and because it involves only the leader, it is a fundamentally autocratic approach. In order to accomplish the task in a more modern and scientific way, we need a **process**. As with any management challenge, the trick is to find a readily identifiable variable that can be measured and driven, i.e. if you can measure it, you can target change in it and influence it positively over time. It will be argued that the key variable in developing organizational culture is **behavior**.

The author has successfully employed the process described here in several corporate situations over a number of years and it works. It is simple to apply and very effective.

The process summarized

Chart 10.0 shows a schematic of the process. It addresses the fact that both the organization and the individual will have their own goals, values and behaviors at the outset. What we are about here is to try to get as much commonality and consistency as possible between these two sets.

As described in previous chapters, the **Leadership Team** will have arrived at a **Mission and Goals** for the organization, with approval from any controlling authority such as a board of directors. This will then be expressed in terms of the **Values** that the organization will need to espouse in order for it to achieve its goals. In turn, the team will identify and target **Behaviors** that they believe will need to be exhibited so as to be consistent with the espoused values. At this point we have something to measure since behavior can be witnessed and recorded.

Goodwill: The Chief Executive's Survival Kit

Executive's Survival Toolkit
**Chart 10.0. Creating Values-Based Corporate Culture –
The Process**

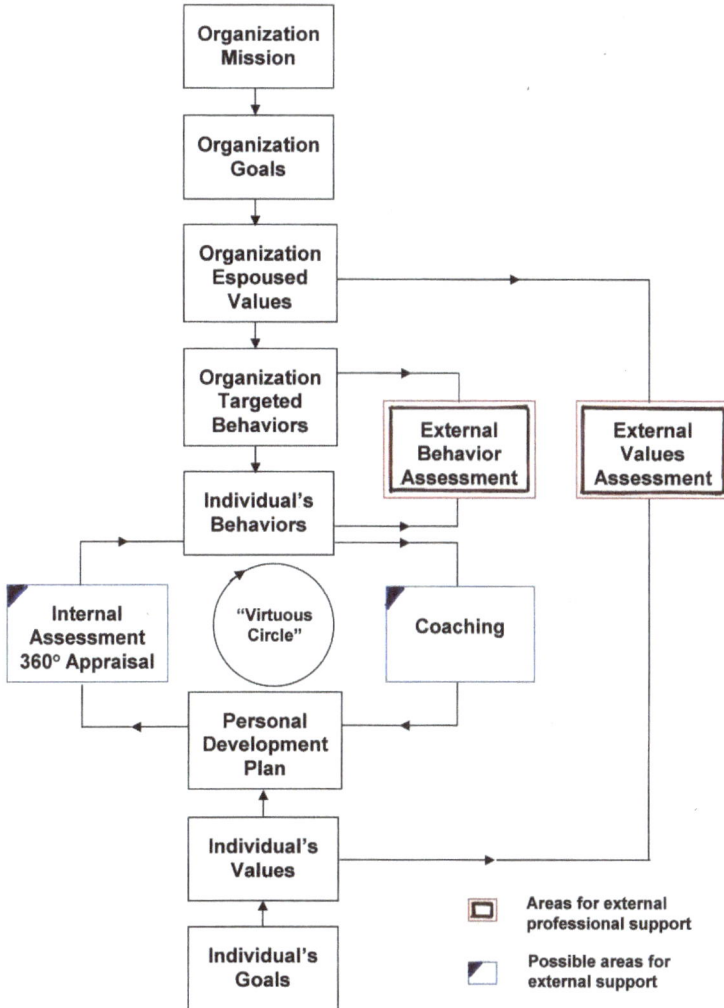

```
          ┌─────────────┐
          │ Organization│
          │   Mission   │
          └─────────────┘
                 │
          ┌─────────────┐
          │ Organization│
          │    Goals    │
          └─────────────┘
                 │
          ┌─────────────┐
          │ Organization│
          │  Espoused   │──────────────────────┐
          │   Values    │                       │
          └─────────────┘                       │
                 │                              │
          ┌─────────────┐     ┌───────────┐    │
          │ Organization│────▶│           │    │
          │  Targeted   │     │  External │  ┌───────────┐
          │  Behaviors  │     │  Behavior │  │ External  │
          └─────────────┘     │ Assessment│  │  Values   │
                 │            └───────────┘  │ Assessment│
          ┌─────────────┐                    └───────────┘
          │ Individual's│───────────────────
          │  Behaviors  │
          └─────────────┘
    ┌──────────┐   ○○○      ┌──────────┐
    │ Internal │  "Virtuous │          │
    │Assessment│   Circle"  │ Coaching │
    │360°Appraisal│  ○○○    │          │
    └──────────┘            └──────────┘
          ┌─────────────┐
          │   Personal  │
          │ Development │
          │    Plan     │
          └─────────────┘
                 │
          ┌─────────────┐
          │ Individual's│
          │   Values    │
          └─────────────┘
                 │
          ┌─────────────┐
          │ Individual's│
          │    Goals    │
          └─────────────┘
```

☐ Areas for external professional support

◣ Possible areas for external support

60

An individual's behavior can be measured against these targeted behaviors and significant deviations identified. For this we use a technique that calls upon a broad sample of feedback from colleagues with whom the individual comes into daily contact called a **360-degree appraisal**. This will be described later.

Armed with this information, the individual is then in a position to put together a **Personal Development Plan (PDP)** that will allow them to address their own behavior style and to mold it so as more closely to reflect that targeted for the organization as a whole. A **Coach** should be selected whose role will be to assist the individual in the preparation and implementation of their PDP. In this way it is possible to steer individuals' behavior towards specific targets and thus, over time, to develop a cohesive and directed culture for the overall organization.

It should be noted that the culture that we are trying to develop should be appropriate for that particular organization in its specific environment at that particular time. We should recognize that this may change over time as the organization develops and changes occur in the environment.

In conjunction with the above, it is most advantageous to assess all key individuals' behavior and values using specialized tools. This will involve bringing in specialists to perform assessments using specially designed instruments. These will ascertain where individuals are not in the right jobs or where they have a fundamentally different value set from the targeted culture and may need to be replaced. If not removed, they are likely to become "blockers" that will undermine the process and hinder the culture development. Behavior and values assessment should also be used in the recruitment process to ensure that people being brought on board have both the skills to perform the particular duties for which they are being recruited but also to ensure that they will fit into and contribute to the developing culture.

Selecting Values consistent with Goals

In Chapter 5, we previously gave an example of a **mission statement** as follows:

"We shall increase customer preference for our brands by exceeding their expectations with superior quality products and services. We shall achieve this through the involvement of all our people and business partners in the continuous improvement of our products, processes, and facilities; thereby sustaining superior financial performance."

The **Goals** associated with this mission statement were:

1. Grow relative market share through improved customer satisfaction whilst maintaining price premium.
2. Involve all our people in the continuous improvement of our business.
3. Simplify the business by focusing on core processes and driving out waste.
4. Improve the contribution and performance of our suppliers.
5. Design and supply defect free product.

These **Goals** can then be translated into a set of **Values** that the **Leadership Team** agrees that the organization must espouse if the goals are to be achieved.

Values, consistent with the goals stated above, in very brief summary might be:

- Mutual respect, trust and integrity
- Empowerment
- Leadership by example
- Effective communication
- Customer focus
- Performance orientation
- Team working

Relating an organization's espoused Values to Behavior

If we take the **Values** identified above, we can identify a consistent set of **Behaviors**. This is presented in Chart 10.1. This can be done by the **Leadership Team** using a brainstorming technique followed by discussion to determine the most important behaviors for each goal, so that a limited and handleable number of behaviors is obtained.

Original painting done by the author

Chart 10.1 Examples of Values with Related Behaviors

Values	Role Model Behaviors
Mutual respect, trust, & integrity	- tell the truth - feedback constructively - keep your promises - support each other
Empowerment	- delegate authority - agree authority limits - welcome new challenges - be proactive
Leadership, by example	- be a role model-whatever your role - be clear about your goals - be passionate about TQM
Effective communication	- listen as well as talk - follow up - use the language of your audience - encourage face-to-face communication
Customer focus	- anticipate stretching targets & consistent & realistic plans - base decisions on facts - celebrate success (recognize and reward)
Team working	- use team working where appropriate - maintain a process orientation (work groups & cross functional work teams) - agree team goals and targets, measure results

Measuring an individual's behaviors against the targeted behaviors

This can be achieved using a short questionnaire that will be completed probably annually by the individual, their immediate boss, several colleagues, several subordinates, and possibly a customer and/or supplier. This is a time consuming exercise, so we need to keep the sample down to about five or six people. An example of such a questionnaire based on the values and behaviors in Chart 10.1 is shown in 10.2. This process is called a **360-degree Appraisal**. It helps if one person in Personnel (or someone who is completely secure from a confidentiality viewpoint) receives all of the responses. If no one exists in the organization, then it is worth going outside. For the purposes of this book, we shall call this person the "**Coordinator**". The Coordinator then adds up the scores and provides feedback in the form of a summary (not specific information) to the individual. The Coordinator or the individual's superior should give this feedback to the individual in person.

The Master's Lodge, Christ's College, Cambridge, England; the author's alma mater.

Goodwill: The Chief Executive's Survival Kit

The Chief Executive's Survival Kit

Chart 10.2 360 - Degree Appraisal Form

Individual being assessed _____   **ASSESSOR: Boss / Peer / Report / Self / Other**
(Please circle)

Value	Behavior	Rating
Mutual Respect, Trust, & Integrity	Shows respect for others	
	Is respected by others	
	Is trusted by others	
	Keeps to his/her promises	
Empowerment	Encourages his/her people to extend their decision-taking scope	
	Agrees the boundaries to which decision taking may be extended	
	Supports people when they explore new ideas, even when things do not go well	
Leadership by Example	Practices what he/she preaches	
	Is decisive	
	Is passionate about Total Quality and continuous improvement	
	Is pro-active	
	Is an effective coach	
	Ensures departmental goals and priorities are clear and understood	
Effective Communication	Is a good listener	
	Articulates messages well	
	Influences others	
	Tailors means of communication to his/her audience	
Customer Focus	Finds out customers' requirements	
	Finds out customers' views or him/her	
	Measures how well he/she satisfies his/her customers	
Performance Orientation	Sets stretching, attainable targets	
	Prioritizes effectively	
	Recognizes success effectively	
	Uses mistakes/failures to initiate future improvements	
Teamworking	chooses effectively when to use a team and when to take individual initiative	
	Works well as a team member	

Behavioral Ratings

Very effective	4
Effective	3
Not very effective	2
Not effective at all	1
Not able to offer a considered opinion	NA

66

The "virtuous circle" and personal development planning

With this summary, the individual can then see where their individual behavior weaknesses lie and put together a personal development plan with a small number of key objectives and an action plan. Ideally, this should also be done with the Coordinator, or alternatively by the individual's superior, who, in this case, must be fully briefed by the Coordinator. This is because they will have access to the make-up of the responses and may be able to detect any bias that may require a specific type of action, for example if the subordinates show very different feedback from colleagues and/or superior.

A **Coach**, whom the individual has nominated and who is acceptable to the individual's superior, may then be selected during this review process. The coach's job will be to monitor progress with the individual regularly, and as often as possible and provide pressure for constructive change. It should be noted that this coach could be almost anyone in the organization who is given the appropriate authority and who is accepted by the individual as suitable.

This process of setting targets, measurement, personal improvement planning, and coaching was designated as a "Virtuous Circle" in Chart 10.0 and shown as a closed loop in the flow chart.

Use of external professionals

Since behavior and values are an essential part of the makeup of the personality of the individual, it is important that the organization has people and teams within it that are compatible with the culture that they are trying to develop. Assessment techniques are now readily available and are Internet accessible. This makes them very simple and inexpensive to use. They are also very accurate and have many years of data contributing to their formulation and veracity.

It is strongly advised that Behavior and Values assessments are undertaken at the very least for the leadership team in order to check that their personality profiles are compatible with the targeted culture and that they will not have to adapt too far outside of their natural style. Operating in a style far removed

from an individual's natural behavioral style has been identified as one of the main contributors to stress at work and ill health. In addition, these assessments can be used to check that the team has the right mix of skills to be a winning combination and will not lead to significant internal conflict and reduced performance. Because of the availability and low cost of these assessment tools, many organizations are now assessing **all** of their employees and their work teams.

At the very least, you should be using these techniques, together with competency assessment that is also now readily available, in the recruitment of all key positions within your organization.

Outside assistance in undertaking these forms of assessment should be used because interpretation of the results requires specialist skills and experience. There are many organizations that currently offer this support. They are also equipped to train your staff to be able to do this in house if you have the internal resources to take this on. You should also consider using external support to coordinate your 360-degree appraisal activity and for follow-up coaching if you do not have the necessary resources internally.

Tower Bridge, London, England

| Chapter 11 | Communicating the Plan and the Compelling Need |

Communicating the plan

No plan is complete without a communication plan to go with it. On many occasions in my own experience, my team and I have spent more time on the communication aspects of a plan than on the plan itself. A good example that comes to mind involved a plant closure. It was essential that we maintained the motivation and commitment of the workforce during a facility closure, largely because we wanted to retain as large a proportion of the skilled people as possible and transfer them to a factory about 40 miles away. We managed to retain about 75 per cent. This was no mean feat and was achieved purely by adequate planning and great communication. At the massed assembly on the factory floor, after I had finished explaining the reasons for the factory closure, how this fitted into the grander scheme of things, and the provisions that would be made for everyone, I was very surprised actually to receive a round of applause. This was most unexpected and I learned a very important lesson right there about the power and importance of good communication.

Even early on in your administration when you have just identified your "**Top Down" Improvement Projects**, these should be widely communicated. As the reader will appreciate, they make much more sense to the workforce when placed against the backdrop of the **Vision, Mission, and Goals**, and **Goal Deployment**. Everyone recognizes that the plan is a dynamic and developing animal and you will get both credit and commitment from your people if you communicate well. They are looking for (and, in my experience, usually crying out for) leadership from you.

Communicating the Compelling Need

Your job as CEO is to communicate The Compelling Need for **change** to the whole company. This is especially important if the changes to the organization and the facilities will be profound such as with a company or divisional Re-structuring or Re-engineering of the operation involving factory closures or significant development as described above.

Remember that, as CEO, you get to recruit and choose your team. If done correctly they will be yours and totally on your side. However, the rest of the organization, including your boss (The Company Chairman) and maybe his peers (other Board members), will have to be persuaded of the need for the changes, and will require a justification for all the costs.

The best way to communicate The Compelling Need and the plans for change to the workforce is to get everyone together at one and the same time. Then, with each member of your team doing his part, explain your intentions to them. Hire the town hall if necessary or some forum that is big enough. Have tea and cakes ready at the end. Do it in several performances if the facility will not hold the whole workforce. Alternatively, if your organization is small, stand up on a table in the middle of the factory floor or office and explain what it is that needs to be done. Do it thoroughly and be completely honest. Do not take questions at this event. This is your event and you must retain complete control. Set up a telephone hotline and a website for people to ask questions and man it with someone else who can speak for the company (not you), or encourage individuals to stop you or any of your **Leadership Team** and ask them.

Do make sure that you deal with rumors, which can be very damaging where significant change is happening in a company. You'll be amazed at some of the rumors that gain currency. Also, bad rumors spread like wildfire. So they must be scotched. My approach was to say publicly that "if anyone has a question, they can get the true story from me or one of my **Leadership Team.** We'll happily tell you. So if I catch anyone spreading untrue and damaging rumors, they will be fired on the spot". That usually did the trick! There is no place for subversive activity in a company that is experiencing significant change.

Be aware that explaining the need for significant change is especially difficult in a company that has historically done extremely well in the past. On one occasion, I ran a company that had done exceptionally well in recent years. It was the market leader in every sense and was the "cash cow" of the group. Because of this, re-investment and development had been neglected and the company had lost its way strategically. To add to its woes, its latest newly introduced consumer product

was not reliable. For this company the compelling need was to define a clear new direction that would deal with the issue of **New Product Development**. Only when new products were truly ready should they be introduced to the market. In this particular case, cost reduction and facilities rationalization was also an important part of the solution. But the more important initiative was an ambitious program of product line simplification and the introduction of a world class **new product development process**. In this particular case, it was just as important to communicate the compelling need for change to the unions and our people if we were to avoid maturation and decline. Needless to say, it was quite a challenge to justify cost saving measures when everyone had witnessed how well the company had done in recent times. As the CEO, this was my responsibility and, through careful planning and good communication, we were able to get everyone behind the leadership team and our strategy and were successful in taking the company to the next level of invincibility.

Communication to The Chairman and The Board will need a different approach with a well presented version of the Strategic Plan and a detailed development plan with all the key projects, funding requirements, timescales and other resources clearly articulated. Make sure that you get them on board. Also, make it clear where your initiatives will be focused and make a point of telling them and agreeing with them at the outset what you are not going to do. Otherwise, you will be bombarded with questions at later reviews such....."what are you doing about so and so". You need to able to say..."we agreed that we would not address that at this stage".

Home Sweet Home (for someone)

| Chapter 12 | Picking the Right Key Performance Indicators |

We cannot manage without measurement. World class companies measure nearly everything. Our task is to make sure that we keep our eye on the essential performance indicators. These will be directly related to our **Goals and our Improvement Projects.**. The **Leadership Team** should assign measurable **Key Performance Indicators** to each and every Goal which will then allow you to measure how you are doing. A realistic **Target** should be set for each performance indicator and the **Actual** compared with the target at least every month. Some performance indicators should be measured quarterly, others annually depending on how quickly change can be effected and the goal achieved.

Examples of **monthly** performance indicators against a goal of "**Improvement Processes**" might be:

- Inventory stock turn
- Overheads as a % of Budget
- Gross value added per employee
- Total warranty claims ($)
- Warranty claims on new products ($)
- Supplier on-time delivery performance
- Supplier quality
- Average first time pass rate
- Scrap/defective product
- Etc.

Examples of **quarterly** performance indicators for the same goal of **Improved Processes** might be:

- Real cost reduction
- New product launch achievement (last 12 months)

An example of an **annual** performance indicator for the same goal might be:

- New Product Development launch cycle time

Chapter 13	Building the Leadership Team to Do the Job

Selecting, developing, and leading a team that is up to the task is the most important challenge for the CEO. You will not be able to succeed on your own! This process needs to be started as soon as you arrive. So, in the early days of your administration, this will be one of your main pre-occupations.

You will probably have inherited an existing team. If not, then you will have to build one. In some ways this is easier because you can start with a blank sheet of paper. Filling the talent gaps in your team's ability will be easier because you will have the opportunity to bring in very strong players from outside.

You may already believe that you have well-honed instincts about people. However, I would strongly advise that you have a professional people person to assist you. In my experience, a good people person can be worth their weight in gold. If you already have a human resources professional, and they are good, stretch them to the full, test them, and use them in assessing the potential of the other members of your Leadership Team. Bring them into your confidence as to what it is that you are trying to do. If they are not up to this task, then to hire a really good people person should be your number one priority.

Alternatively, and I have done this in situations where I have not had the right HR person or where they are not yet ready for the task, go outside and get some help from a strategy consultant or an executive search consultant whose judgment you trust and who is prepared to get deeply inside your head and your business. Let this person work with you, attend meetings (especially the **Team Purpose Analysis, Vision, Mission and Goals, Goal Deployment, etc.**), and spend time with each of your potential Leadership Team members so that they will be able to get into a position of being able to have meaningful discussions with you about your peoples' capability and where you have gaps that must be filled.

It makes good sense to use employees who have been with the organization for some time and to recruit from within. However, if the organization is sick and you have been brought in to make radical changes, be aware that they may be a major part of the

problem and be ready to make radical changes at the Leadership Team level. It is often true that the kinds of changes to the business that you may wish to make may be just too big for some of the existing players.

If and when you get to the point of accepting that you need to bring in top notch people from outside to fill senior positions, you should consider using an executive search firm. I have found it helpful in my career to be close to a small number of outstanding executive search individuals who get to know you as a CEO and understand exactly what you expect from them and the quality of people that you are likely to be looking for.

You should regard this search exercise in a similar manner to **benchmarking**. Identify the job profile as precisely as you can and also specify the type of person who would fit the bill. Then ask yourself the question whether it is likely that you will find anyone in the industry in which your business competes who can deliver the level of out-of-the-box thinking and excellence that you are looking for. If the answer is yes and the best performing companies in your sector have good people, it will be a relatively straightforward task for the headhunter to go after them. If the answer is no, as is usually the case, select industries where they have already achieved a level of excellence far in advance of your industry (e.g. automotive, electronics, retailing, etc.) where individuals are likely to be operating with the level of competence that you are seeking in the particular areas that you have specified, and work with the executive search firm to research these industries closely for talent.

In the USA, there is a predisposition to try to find people with experience within a particular industry. This is not the case in Europe where it is considered to be very advantageous to bring talented people into an unfamiliar industry in order that they add significant value to this new sector from their experience and particular expertise in another. In my own case, I have operated in many different industry sectors and have never found it difficult to migrate very rapidly from one to the other. There may be exceptions, but lack of specific industry knowledge is seldom a constraint for very long to a really good manager experienced in other industries. So do not be afraid to cast the net far and wide.

Where you are bringing in someone new into a position that in title may already be filled but by someone who is not big enough for the job as you now envision it, unless they are part of the problem, try to be creative in finding for them a function that they can fulfill. In this way, you do not lose their experience to the organization or to a competitor. You will have a selling job to do, of course, to get them to accept what they may see as a demotion. But if you are clear enough in your thinking about what you are trying to achieve, you should be able to get the message across. In my experience, they may even be relieved not to have to take on the much greater responsibility that you will require for the job that you want done. As always, good communication is of the essence.

One final thought. I have spent a good deal of time in this section describing the importance of a good people person. The most successful example that I have witnessed of a CEO bringing a large, traditional organization out of the dark ages and completely revitalizing it with new talent and new ways of operating involved a CEO and a people person working "in tandem". The people person provided a constant stream of the best people from a range of different industries and the CEO deployed them hither and thither in their areas of competence. The result was incredible to behold and brought about a complete transformation of a major public company in a matter of just a few years. The CEO could not have done it without the people person being "joined at the hip" with him. In this case, executive search firms were used who were closely managed by line management and the people person.

A summary of key elements towards building the right leadership team to do the job is given in Checklist Number 5.

Checklist Number 5
Building the Leadership Team to do the Job

Key Elements:

- Assess Leadership Team using

    1. Psychological Testing

    2. Experience and "gut" feel

- Remove "Blockers" and Poor Performers swiftly

- Recruit "Stars" from Parallel, Top-Performing, Benchmarked Industries

- Challenge Individuals to Prepare their Department's Plan and Budget and Task Realistically

- Perform Monthly One-on-One Performance Reviews of Direct Reports Against Personal Performance Goals

- Conduct 360 % Appraisal Annually Against PDP (Personal Development Plan) Based on Values/Behavior Criteria for Company Culture Development

- Be a Good Coach

- Get a Good Coach Yourself

The Road Home, Mentone, Alabama.

76

| **Chapter 14** | **Identify and Focus on Core Activities** |

Every Leadership Team should identify what are the **Core Activities** for its business. Some of these will be the same for businesses in different sectors. Others will be very sector specific. When they have been identified, it is the CEO's job to drive **Continuous Improvement** initiatives to make the company World Class in these Core Activities.

One fairly specific example that I can quote involves the shower company that I have already used as an example. They used brass castings for the "engine" of their shower temperature and flow controller. These castings had a lot of subsequent machining, which was expensive. They were chromed and very decorative in the final product. To find a defect, which effectively rendered it scrap, in a casting after it had been submitted to a lot of machining was very expensive. The company had decided that it was not in the brass casting business, which is very specialized, and had closed down its foundry. Casting was not considered a core activity. It was forced to change its mind because, even on a worldwide scale the supply of high integrity, defect-free castings in relatively small numbers (hundreds of thousands of units rather than millions) is extremely limited. So they were forced to admit that brass casting was a core skill and they are now back in the casting business! This is a good example of where, as a CEO, you need to know your core processes.

Chart 14.0 shows typical Core Activities and how they should be approached.

CHART 14.0 FOCUS ON CORE ACTIVITIES

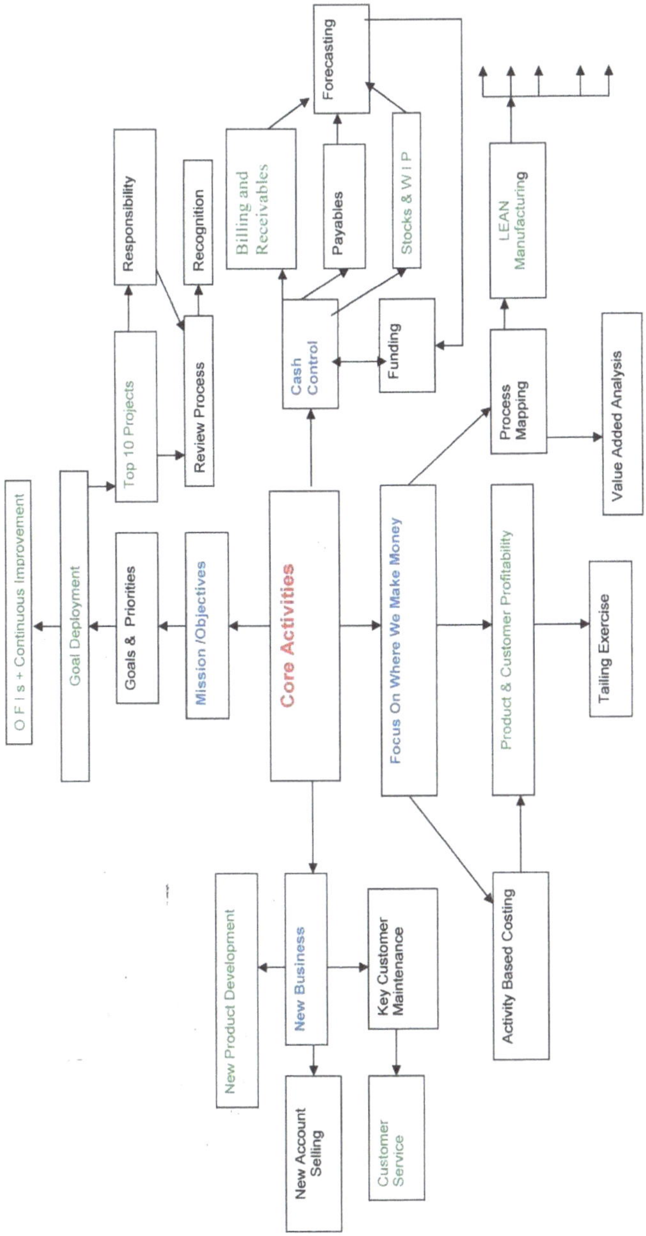

- O F I s + Continuous Improvement
- Goal Deployment
- Top 10 Projects
- Review Process
- Responsibility
- Recognition
- Goals & Priorities
- Mission /Objectives
- Core Activities
- Billing and Receivables
- Forecasting
- Payables
- Stocks & W I P
- Cash Control
- Funding
- LEAN Manufacturing
- Focus On Where We Make Money
- Process Mapping
- Value Added Analysis
- Product & Customer Profitability
- Tailing Exercise
- New Product Development
- New Business
- Key Customer Maintenance
- New Account Selling
- Customer Service
- Activity Based Costing

The following list provides examples of core processes for the average business:

- Goal Deployment
- Budgeting and Budgetary Control
- Continuous Improvement (Kaizen)
- Top Down Priority Improvement Projects Identification and Implementation
- Project Management
- Cash Control
- Focus on where we make Money – Product and Customer Profitability
- Lean Manufacturing
- New Business Development
- New Product Development
- Customer Service
- Inventory Control
- Lean Manufacturing

Any business that does all these well will maximize its likelihood of success and optimize its profit potential.

An English Village Green.

Chapter 15	How to Grow Profit

Chart 15.0 provides a roadmap that shows schematically how profits can be grown.

The three core areas are **Business Unit Focus**, **Complexity Reduction**, and **Improved Margins**. Each of these will spawn projects in the areas shown above and below the three core areas. Those shown above relate to products and marketing; those below to manufacturing and production. Several of the topics mentioned are dealt with in other chapters of this book. It is not the intention here to go over all the topics. But this chart can be helpful in that it illustrates how the various action areas all fit together in a logical sequence to generate **Profit Growth**. It is a very useful communication aid to get the Leadership Team all thinking in unison and all on the same page.

This roadmap has been used successfully in several businesses. (see Page 81)

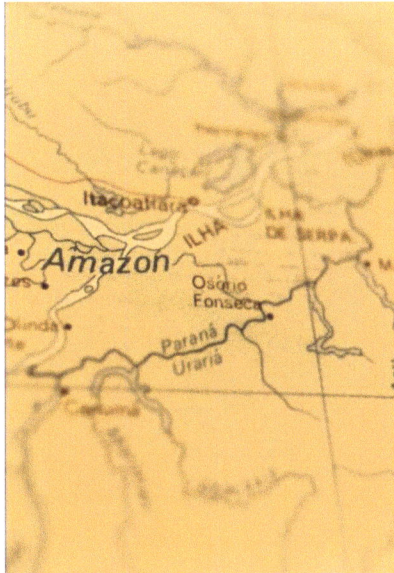

Chart 15.0

How to Grow Profits - The Roadmap

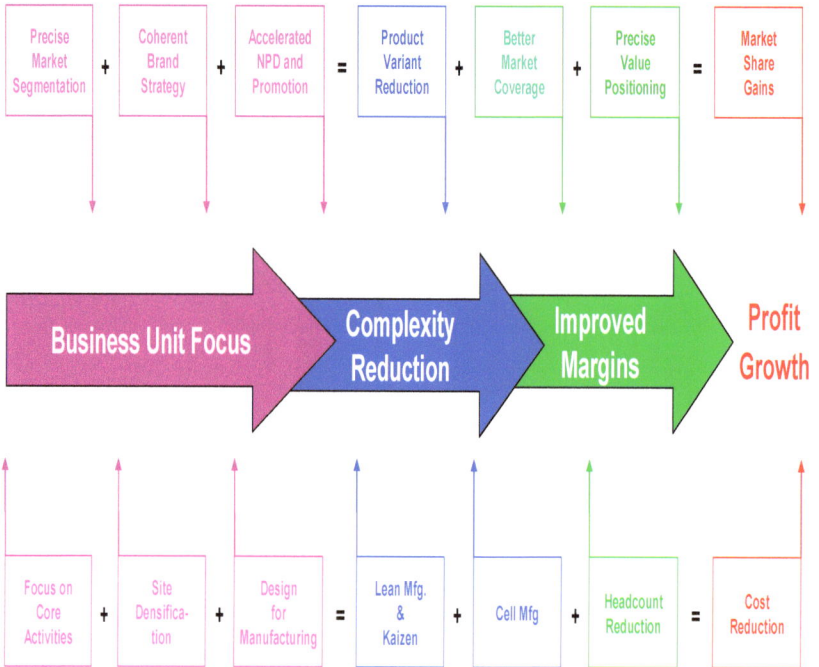

| Precise Market Segmentation | + | Coherent Brand Strategy | + | Accelerated NPD and Promotion | = | Product Variant Reduction | + | Better Market Coverage | + | Precise Value Positioning | = | Market Share Gains |

Business Unit Focus → Complexity Reduction → Improved Margins → Profit Growth

| Focus on Core Activities | + | Site Densifica- tion | + | Design for Manufacturing | = | Lean Mfg. & Kaizen | + | Cell Mfg | + | Headcount Reduction | = | Cost Reduction |

Dr. David J. Goodwill 1995

Chapter 16 | Complexity Reduction

Organizations become very complex over time. The secret is to eradicate or minimize the impact of non core processes; and to identify clearly all the **core processes** (as described in a previous chapter), and to take action to simplify these. Here are some areas to look out for.

THE ORDER BOOK

As described in Chapter 4 and "Where do we make money?", the Pareto Principle applies to the order book. If you have not done a "tailing exercise" recently you will find that at least 80% of your business is in the top 20% when measured by size of order plotted against number of orders. Make a decision not to take orders below a certain size and cut out the long "tail" of your order book.

On one memorable occasion, I challenged my team to come up with a plan to cut off 40 % of the order book (the "tail") in terms of number of orders. This was an entirely arbitrary target and one that I thought would be extremely challenging. I knew that it would get resistance from the Sales Department, so I made the VP of Sales and Marketing the Sponsor of the project. He and his project team surprised and delighted me when they came back with the answer that we should cut out 50% of the order book in terms of number of orders, and have a slightly smaller but much more profitable business. This was a good lesson in tasking a project team. I have to say that the organization that this refers to was exceptional and an extremely effective TQM company with a "can do" attitude unequalled in my experience.

CUSTOMER PROFITABILITY

Plot the average price or average unit financial contribution versus order size by customer for your whole order book. Obviously the most profitable orders are the large orders with the highest average price or unit financial contribution. You want as many of these as you can get. However, in a mature business you will find many that are small in size and unit contribution. Worse still, you will find many that are large in size with only a small financial contribution. Try to increase prices on the lowest financial contribution items. If you lose the business, it will have

little impact on the bottom line but will have a significant impact on the complexity of your business and greatly simplify the challenge in manufacturing and production.

DESIGN ENGINEERING

Redesign your products so as to utilize common components. When I took over a door and window company recently, the products had been designed by architects. Every patio door and window product had different sized screws and fixtures. The manufacturing engineers were able to redesign the products over time so as to utilize common parts. This reduced inventory and greatly simplified manufacturing processes.

PROCESS MAPPING

Map all your key processes (especially the core processes) including staff activities. Teach your personnel to do this so that they can map their own area. Then remove all unnecessary elements or retain but simplify core activities. Encourage employees to come up with OFIs...Opportunities For Improvement. Offer recognition rewards for complexity reduction and efficiency improvements.

LEAN MANUFACTURING

Set up teams of manufacturing engineers whose role is to examine whole areas of the factory with a view to re-engineering your manufacturing operation. Establish budgets to do this. See also the chapter entitled "Lean Manufacturing".

An Indian Chief's Face in the Mountain?

TIME MANAGEMENT

Get all staff personnel to keep a log of how they spend their time. Encourage them to set targets for each essential activity and stick to those targets and not get distracted or drawn into someone else's problems. This is especially true for you, the CEO. You will have the hardest time doing this but you must stick to your targets. The secret for you has several elements:

- Recruit competent direct reports who you can trust
- Delegate as much as you possibly can to them
- Give them clear targets
- Make sure they understand the limits of their authority and the circumstances under which they should refer back to you
- Support and protect them when they need it to build their self confidence
- Get out of their way!

MEETINGS

Meetings can completely bog down an organization because it's much easier to talk than to do. Set an example to the rest of the organization by making sure that your meetings are short and sweet and well managed (See also the later chapter "Meetings Management").

"Big Ben" in London, England

Chapter 17 | Lean Manufacturing

Lean Manufacturing emphasizes the optimization of systems, people, machines, materials, and facilities. This is a very specialist area requiring specialist and properly qualified engineers. If you believe that your business would benefit from a thorough **re-engineering** exercise, you will need either to bring in consultants or recruit manufacturing engineers or both. If you decide to recruit, look to industries that use manufacturing engineers on a regular basis in product design and manufacturing. The obvious example would be the automotive industry. You cannot grow this skill in house. Bring in specialists who know how to do this stuff already. You will also need to embark on a training exercise for the rest of your organization so that everyone understands what re-engineering and lean manufacturing is all about. Be ready for major culture shifts. What these guys do will fundamentally change your business. Also be ready to pay them well. They are the highest paid profession on the corporate scene and good ones are really sought after.

It is beyond the scope of this book to cover all the things that your manufacturing engineers will bring to your business but here are some examples:

- High performance manufacturing culture

- Empowered team approach

- Multi-skilling

- Kaizen (Continuous Improvement)

- Optimized plant layout

- Cellular manufacturing

- Single piece work flow / continuous flow

- Localized quality control

- Minimized inventory and work in process (WIP)

- Strategic partnerships with suppliers [inventory at suppliers, just-in-time (JIT), Kanbans, etc.]

Goodwill: The Chief Executive's Survival Kit

- Reduction of floor space / spare capacity
- Total productive maintenance (TPM)
- 5 "S"
- Minimized lead times
- Greatly enhanced efficiency

"Shoot for the Moon"
(photo by Dr. Sharon Goodwill)

| Chapter 18 | New Product Development |

The Process

New Product Development (NPD) is all about the process and should be managed as such. It should be an area of **Core Competence**. Without a very tightly managed process, the introduction of new products can cause chaos to every part of the organization.

If you believe your NPD process is not top notch, undertake a **benchmarking** exercise to find an organization with similar needs to your own that has a **world class NPD process** and go talk with them. Organizations that are world class are nearly always delighted to share their knowledge and expertise. Then "steal shamelessly" and put their process into your organization. A world class NPD process will involve **tollgates**. These require that everything be signed off at each stage of the process (literally and "in blood") before the project can move on to the next stage in the process. This avoids everything getting pushed to the last moment with design engineers still doing their thing when the product launch date is rapidly approaching!

WW II Memorial, Thames Embankment, London.

The key tollgate phases are:

1. Identify and test market the opportunity
2. Be clear about what the user/customer values and will pay for
3. Design
4. Test manufacture
5. Manufacture
6. Launch

Everyone in your organization should receive **training** in New Product Development. The extent of their training should be tailored to their involvement in the NPD process itself. The normal rules about good **project management** that were dealt with in a previous chapter apply. Indeed the project management structure illustrated in Chart 9.1 of Chapter 9 is precisely the organization that you should aim for.

It is my experience that the most successful NPD teams are "**trios**". A trio is a team comprising a marketing person, a design engineer, and a manufacturing engineer. Each plays a lead role in the project at different points in the process. The **review process** previously discussed also applies. Project progress should be reviewed on a regular basis at least every month. As CEO you should be involved personally in all aspects of the NPD process. If a new product fails, it will be your head on the block!

One last tip…do not allow your engineers to introduce more than one **new technology** into a new product. By new technology I mean a technology that is unfamiliar to your company. This is usually more than your organization will be able to handle and is asking for trouble. In general, NPD should be an evolutionary process building on prior product knowledge and experience, not a revolutionary one.

| Chapter 19 | **Cash Management** |

Cash flow Forecasting and Management should always be core competencies in any business. Even successful and very profitable businesses can fail because they run out of cash. This tends to happen where very high growth is experienced and the business does not have enough cash from the lower level of sales to pay for rapidly increasing requirements in raw materials and labor. Rapidly growing businesses always require continual injections of **working capital** unless the product is paid for up-front or in stage payments, which occurs in the building sector and some high tech industries. Make sure that **cash flow** becomes as important a topic at your regular management meetings as **profit and loss** and **balance sheet – related** items.

Setting tight **payment criteria** (days payable) and managing **receivables** very tightly are two key elements of cash management. The sales force needs to be as adept at getting the right payment criteria as they are at getting the best price for the product. Regarding receivables, this is a specialist area and requires a specialist to do it. Make sure your organization has such a person. Also, ensure that Sales and Accounting Departments work together on receivables so that poorly paying customers are "weeded out" and the problem does not grow to an insurmountable level for individual customers.

Seasonal considerations also need to be taken into account. Most businesses have some seasonal element. The key here is to have access to an adequate **line of credit** with your bank(s) to get you over the seasonal peaks in demand.

Chapter 20 — Meetings Management

Meetings take up a lot of time and sap the creative energy of your people if not controlled and managed. You should make sure that you are not the problem! Get feedback from your Leadership Team as to the competence of your meetings management style. It is my experience that people can lose respect for their boss over this more than any other single reason.

Here are some rules for **Meetings Management** that should be adhered to absolutely and become sacrosanct within your organization.

1. Post the **Meeting Rules** in the meeting room clearly visible. Keep them concise, and clear.

2. Set a **time**, **place**, and **duration** (not more than one hour).

3. Embarrass **latecomers**; get them to make a donation to the "late box"

4. For quick meetings do not let anyone **sit** down.

5. Circulate an **agenda** at least 24 hours in advance.

6. At the beginning of each meeting appoint a **Facilitator** to control the agenda and timing, and a **Scribe** to record decisions.

7. The **Chairman** controls the content of the meeting and ensures that all attendees contribute.

8. Only **one person** speaks at a time.

9. **Mutual respect** must be maintained at all times.

10. Ideally, the scribe should record decisions on an **electronic blackboard** so that attendees leave the meeting with a copy of the meeting **minutes and action points**.

11. Each **action point** should have the **name** of the person responsible for that action.

12. Agree on time and place for any **follow up** meeting.

13. End the meeting **on time**.

French Flag on Paris rooftop in France.

| Chapter 21 | The Power of Recognition |

eople respond very favorably to being given a "**thank you**" for a job well done. As discussed in an earlier chapter, It is one of the key roles of the CEO to manage the **Recognition Process** and have a very high visibility in it. This is the business of celebrating success. As CEO you want to be seen to be associated with success.

The process should be formalized into a **Recognition Calendar** issued at the beginning of the year with events planned and executed every month, and with impromptu events as needed. **Recognition Rewards** need not be expensive. The perceived value of the award to the employee far outways the cost to the organization. A certificate or plaque or a trophy, ideally manufactured in your own machine shop, are good rewards, together with an all-expenses-paid dinner for two at a prominent, local restaurant. An arrangement can be negotiated with the owner of the restaurant to get a really good price for all-included meals for, say, twenty couples over the next twelve months. It is amazing how motivating it is for an employee to have a recognition reward that they are able to share with their partner or spouse.

An **Employee of the Month** program works well where the best **Opportunity For Improvement (OFI)** is recognized and celebrated. This program might be conducted as follows:

- The **OFIs** are tendered by department heads in writing on a form designed for the purpose

- A **committee** selected from throughout the company for this purpose should choose the best OFI each month against agreed criteria

- The winning individual or team receives the award from the CEO at the pre-planned **Recognition Event**

- The event is **published** on the notice boards and employees are encouraged to attend

- The Event is covered in the local newspaper and/or company **newspaper**.

As already covered in a previous chapter, the CEO should also hold **breakfasts** and **brown bag lunches** at least once a week with groups of about ten people. It is amazing how people will open up once they see that it is safe to do so. This is a great way for you to get to know what is really going on in your company and to gauge the morale and attitudes of the employees.

Boating on the River Cam in Cambridge, England.

| **Chapter 22** | **Twelve Traits of Successful Leaders** |

Here are 12 traits often associated with successful leaders:

1. **A Powerful Presence:** The ability to create trust and instill confidence in people.

2. **A Dream and Vision:** Define the purpose and the destination.

3. **Focus and Discipline:** Insist on scientific principles and measurement. Set goals and objectives. Review them regularly.

4. **Recognition and Encouragement**: Celebrate success on a regular, scheduled basis.

5. **Intellectual Creativity:** Rethink old problems in new ways, and help others to do the same.

6. **Moral Courage and Integrity:** Willingness to stand up for ideas, people and what's right. Be the role model.

7. **Reliability:** Keep promises and commitments, and accept responsibility for your actions. Insist others do the same.

8. **Adaptability:** Embrace change; be flexible.

9. **People**: Hire the right people and put them in their best jobs. Delegate as much as you possibly can and push responsibility and accountability downwards.

10. **Judgment and Decision Making:** Consider relevant points of view, decide on a preferred course, and then act. Communicate your decision.

11. **Respect:** Treat all people with the same consideration, regardless or their rank or position.

12. **Sense of Humor:** Look at life with humor and a degree of personal humility.

| Chapter 23 | Useful Hints Regarding Acquisitions |

If your strategy involves an acquisition, this is a very specific area of management activity, fraught with challenges, that requires particular knowledge and skill. Checklist 6 below provides some useful hints.

Checklist 6: Ten Key Hints on Acquisitions

1. Both parties must have the authority and <u>want</u> to do the deal.

2. Compromise is necessary and inevitable during negotiation.

3. The principals should agree a "terms sheet" with no lawyers present.

4. Then the lawyers can add the details.

5. Use a lawyer who is commercially savvy.

6. Price is seldom the most difficult issue.

7. Representations (Reps.) and Warranties are always tough.

8. As the deal progresses, expect a "roller coaster" ride.

9. Be prepared "to walk" if necessary.

10. Remember – it's not personal; it's just business. Ongoing good relationships with former owners can be very advantageous to you.

| Chapter 24 | **Further observations** |

Here are a few final thoughts and observations:

- The **industry** you adopt is the single most important factor for profit – choose a high growth, lucrative sector where competition is immature or limited.

- Dominate the **premium sector** of the market, where possible.

- The most successful organizations often have a successful **management duo**.
  e.g. CEO & CFO
       CEO & VP Human Resources
       Entrepreneur plus professional manager.

- Major **metro areas** have the right characteristics for incubating new and successful companies.
  - Networks.
  - Universities / smart people.
  - Funding sources.
  - Etc, etc.

- Good **cash flow forecasting** is essential to any business.

- Don't depend on **bankers** making logical decisions.

- It is impossible to manage without **measurement**.

- Your **people** will make the difference; choose them well and train them so that they maximize their full potential.

- Know when to **hold 'em**, know when to **fold 'em**, know when to **walk away**, and know when to **run**!

- Good **planning** is essential--- don't get the Christopher Columbus award for management.....he started off not knowing where he was going and came back not knowing where he had been!

Appendix: List of Charts and Checklists